GET STUFF DONE

THE GSD FACTOR

STUDENT
WORKBOOK

MISHA
BLEYMAIER-FARRISH

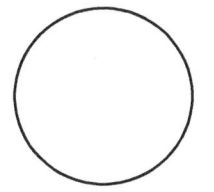
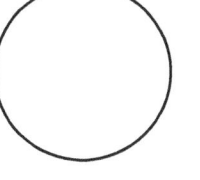
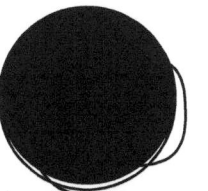
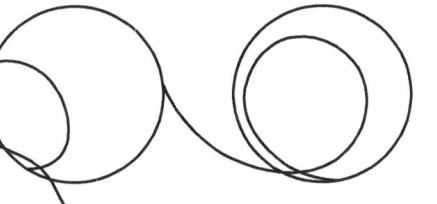
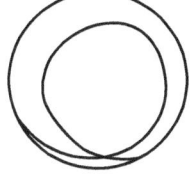

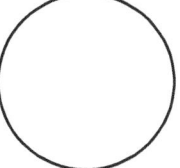

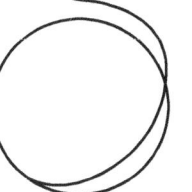
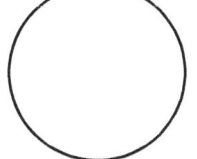

GSD®

FACTOR \ PUBLISHING

Published by
GSD Factor Publishing
www.gsdfactor.com
info@gsdfactor.com
6688 Nolensville Road, Ste. 108-107
Brentwood, TN 37027-8833

Printed in the United States of America

GSD Factor LLC and GSD Factor Publishing LLC are committed to human-generated content. This book was developed, written, and edited by humans without the assistance of artificial intelligence.

A special thanks to the GSD Factor Publishing Team:
Book Coach + Editor-in-Chief: Qualia C. Hendrickson
Editor: Alacia Reynolds
Cover Design: Ella Carlton Shirk
Interior Design: Carla Green
Author Headshot: Mat Brown

ISBN 979-8-9877272-9-4 (paperback)

To our future GSDers:

Learn from our successes and mistakes.
Learn what to do, but more importantly, what not to do.
Live authentically.
Be the change makers that you are meant to be.
We are cheering you on!

To: _____

Message: _____

_____

_____

_____

_____

_____

_____

Belongs to: _____

Email: _____

CONTENTS

Introduction 1

ATTRIBUTE ONE:

BE CONFIDENT 5

    This Is Me 9

    Your True Authentic Self 13

    Use Your Voice 19

    Passion And Dedication 23

ATTRIBUTE TWO:

BE INQUISITIVE 31

    Always Learn Something 35

    GSD Factor Squad 41

ATTRIBUTE THREE:

BE IMAGINATIVE 53

    Dream Big 57

    Never Be Satisfied 61

    Problems Lead to Solutions 67

ATTRIBUTE FOUR:

BE PRESENT 79

    Keep Showing Up 83

    Progress Not Perfection 87

    Be Present 93

    Pivot Decisions 97

ATTRIBUTE FIVE:

BE RESILIENT 105

    Resilient Life 109

    Trust the Timing 119

    Perspective 123

ATTRIBUTE SIX:

BE INFLUENTIAL 129

    Leader by Example 133

    Challenging the Stereotypes 139

    Heroes + Sheroes + Mentors 141

    THE GSD FACTOR LIFE 145

7

INTRODUCTION

The day had come. December 31st, hours before the ball dropped to signify the coming new year. While everyone else in the country was celebrating with family, my team and I were adding the final touches to our audit. Think of an audit like your senior-year exams. Tests like the SATs or ACTs, can determine which college you attend, your scholarship eligibility, and your future path. Well, this audit was exactly that for me, my team, and my organization. There was only one grade: pass or fail, and failure meant that I was out of a job.

For six weeks, my team and I worked crazy hours under immense pressure and managed to complete one of the most complicated and intense financial exams our company had encountered. The crazy thing, though, is that my superiors, the people who should have been rooting for my success, seemed to be hoping for the opposite. You may think bullies only exist in middle or high school, but friend, let me tell you: they exist when you are an adult as well.

At this point in my life, I was really struggling. I had come off of a break to find my job different than it had been before. I had returned to such an immense amount of work and pressure, that after a while, the only conclusion I could come to was that my company was working to make me quit or take my job away, whichever came first. So, when they assigned me a massive project at the end of the year, I knew that they all assumed I would fail.

It was, essentially, an impossible project, because the timeline was impractical. This was the type of project that could take years to complete, and yet my bosses assigned it the week leading into national holidays, and it was due on New Year's Day. Can you imagine studying for the SATs or ACTs in just six weeks with Thanksgiving (a US holiday), Christmas, New Year's Day and the other holidays being celebrated in the same time period? There was no way it would happen, and they knew it. Additionally, because it was an exam that was so important to the organization, they knew that when it failed, they would have reason to take my job away.

What they didn't expect, however, was that I would use this as motivation. I am really good at getting stuff done, or as I like to say, "GSDing." This project, though meant to break me, simply stirred a deep passion to prove them wrong. This was dedication in action, and I was going to GSD.

During that time, I only took Thanksgiving Day and Christmas Day off. On Christmas Eve, my team and I were working. On weekends, we were working. My team knew what was at stake. They saw the bullying and said, "We run with you; just tell us how fast." And guess what? We delivered. We made the deadline. On New Years' Day, I submitted the completed exam with all corresponding paperwork to the surprise of my boss. Not only did we meet all the expectations of the exam, the auditor grading this exam said that it was the best run, best laid out, and most organized exam and project he had ever been through over his 30-year career.

That experience, though challenging, is only one of many similar situations that I've faced in my life, situations that pushed me beyond my physical, emotional, and mental limits. Challenges like this have required me to pull from many different places to achieve success. In those moments, I channel the strength and ingenuity of my family. I refer back to all the lessons my parents taught me, all the times I had been counted out because of gender, age, educational status, or physical impairments. All of these combined experiences ultimately made me who I am–a woman who knows how to get stuff done–my life's motto.

Now, when I say "get stuff done," I'm not trying to coin a catchphrase or hashtag. It's more than that. The GSD Factor ignites a transformation in your life. It's an attitude that helps you accomplish seemingly insurmountable feats. It's a mindset that helps you cultivate an unshakeable confidence in your identity and your abilities. It's about practical execution. I believe that every single one of us has the GSD Factor within us, but maybe, for some of you, it just hasn't been activated or needs to be reignited. Do you consistently find yourself in situations where you feel like an "other" or an "only" because of your gender, age, ethnicity, or simply because you march to the beat of your own drum? Maybe you're a dreamer who's constantly looking for ways to improve or questioning how things have always been. If you inspire others with your resilience or courage and ability to be fully present in all situations, or if you often feel drawn to lead and to use your voice to influence others, then the GSD Factor drive is active in you.

Now that we've established the GSD Factor, here's a little about me. My name is Misha Bleymaier-Farrish. I'm an author, entrepreneur, founder, career coach, speaker, military-family member, non-profit organization board member, mentor, wife, and mother. I'm an advocate for the under-voiced, mentoring the next generation of leaders and equipping those that may need direction and clarity. As you can tell, I wear many hats. I've been blessed with many talents, and I honor those blessings by making sure I'm operating as efficiently, authentically, smoothly, and purposefully as possible. I get stuff done because I don't want to waste or squander the gifts that have been given to me.

Anyone who knows me, knows that I love to dream big, question the status quo, and just GSD. My team would tell you I'm the GSD boss. My kids would tell you I'm the GSD Momma. Some have even said, about me: "There goes Misha, GSDing!"

Throughout my life, I've always been known as a person who could execute, under pressure or otherwise. I realized fairly early that my problem solving skills and ability to find success in challenging situations didn't come so easily to everyone. I constantly find myself meeting people and almost instantly being asked for advice with a difficult task or problem. My experiences birthed this GSD mindset, and the benefits of GSD living motivate me to share this concept with others, including you, my friends.

I know what you're thinking: What is the GSD Factor? Why do I need it, and how will having a GSD mindset help me in the future? There are six keys, or as I like to say, attributes that come to mind. To live the GSD Factor lifestyle, you must:

1. Be Confident

2. Be Inquisitive

3. Be Imaginative

4. Be Present

5. Be Resilient

6. Be Influential

Someone with an activated GSD Factor has the confidence or boldness to know their true, authentic self and their own voice and has the assertiveness to speak their truth and be heard. They have the humility to be inquisitive. They ask lots of questions and know that they are not the smartest people in the room, but they have the ability to bring together the right team to ensure that they are open to the fullness of life. They're imaginative or think about things differently and are not afraid to dream big. They're never satisfied with how things have always been done, and say, "I'm here. What can we make better? What is impossible that we can make possible?" They know to be present or be still and trust the process even when it seems that there are more changes than plans. They have the stamina, grit, and perseverance to acknowledge that life can be hard sometimes and the resilience or courage to turn the negatives into positives. Finally, they have influence. They lead by example, look to the future, and bring teammates along with them. These six attributes are the foundational principles from which all other aspects of the GSD Factor develop. They are the attributes that I have cultivated throughout my lifetime and the ones that I find in common with other GSDers I've encountered along my journey.

HOW TO READ THIS BOOK

Throughout this book, the GSD Factor attributes and the personal lessons from my life's experiences are woven into the chapters. My hope is that these stories will encourage and empower you to activate the GSD Factor within you. I'm not only a strong believer that you can learn something from any experience; I'm walking evidence that it is true. Hopefully my stories or your own experiences, provide some guidance on what to do and what not to do.

There are questions, journal prompts, or activities throughout this workbook. These are there to help you think about the GSD Factor attributes and train you on how to use them in your life. You will always need confidence, inquisitiveness, imagination, presence, resilience, and influence. So, why not learn now? The sooner you learn these, the faster you will be able to face anything that life throws at you. You may have already had some struggles, and if that is the case, hopefully these stories and activities will remind you of how awesome you are. Think of it like a high five, pat on the back, or a big hug. I'm rooting for you. You've got this. I'm so proud of you.

The other important thing to remember is that whoever gifted this book to you is one of your biggest fans or cheerleaders. They see you. They hear you. They want to make sure that you have the right tools to be the greatest version of you there can be. Be sure to talk to them if you have any questions or if any of our topics don't make any sense. Remember you are not alone.

The biggest thing is to connect with other GSDers that are walking your same journey. Your parents, grandparents, family members, teachers, coaches, other leaders that love and care for you. Share and learn together; laugh and cry, and know you are not alone. I am grateful that you have chosen to embark on this journey with me. Let's stay connected, so we can collaborate to harness the power of teamwork, or as we like to say here: Let's GSD! Welcome to your GSD Factor life, friend.

ATTRIBUTE ONE

BE **CONFIDENT**

Being confident means being bold enough to be yourself in a world that constantly wants you to conform.

> Obstacles don't have to stop you. If you run into a wall, don't turn around and give up. Figure out how to climb it, go through it, or work around it.

– MICHAEL JORDAN

ACTIVITY

Fill out this sentence:

My name is _____,

and I'm a _____

_____

_____

_____

_____

_____

(It can be multiple things such as student, athlete, artist, daughter, son, etc.).

BE CONFIDENT

THE POWER AND CONFIDENCE IN KNOWING YOUR TRUE AUTHENTIC SELF, KNOWING YOUR VOICE, AND SPEAKING YOUR TRUTH SO THAT YOU ARE HEARD.

1

THIS IS ME

When I was nine, I traveled with my dad to The Frankfurt Book Fair in Germany. Every year, thousands of people attend the week-long event to showcase their latest books and make connections. At the time, Dad was the vice president of international sales for books and music for a contemporary Christian publishing and music company. He attended the fair every year and was an incredible networker. Dad knew how to talk to everyone and had a natural talent for connecting with people, and he could easily spot that same gift in others. Dad would later tell me how he saw that ability to connect with people in me at an early age, especially if they were sick or injured. Instances like that showed him that I not only had a special concern for helping people, but I also had a confidence that gave me boldness and courage to talk to anyone. Looking back at it, I believe that he must have specifically taken me on this trip to ignite that confidence in me.

On this particular trip, he saw my sales and networking potential and decided to give me an opportunity to hone that skill set. My job was to read every new release that we were showcasing and be able tell people about it. Sounds pretty easy, right? Maybe for an adult who had years of training and experience in sales, but I was nine! Still, even at nine years old, I knew that if I didn't put myself out there, I wouldn't make the connections that I needed. Dad knew that too, and he prepared me for how to engage with people. We prepared talking points for each book. He taught me to make eye contact, smile, and then speak so that people would come into my booth and want to learn more. Dad also prepared me for rejection by telling me that it was a normal thing. He emphasized that I would have to get through a "no" to get to a "yes," and I quickly realized that the faster you get through the "no," the better!

That day, I made my way around to the other booths, introducing myself and getting to know the neighbors. I talked about the books Dad brought and whatever else I could think of. Thankfully, I had my dad's gift of gab, so the conversation flowed freely. I was definitely the only kid there. Looking back on the experience, I can see how I naturally realized the importance of connecting with people. It's not hard to find commonalities with people; it just takes effort. I was able to engage with people and navigate those interactions effortlessly. Even if I was faced with a no, I went back one more time to see if I could win them over. If I could, great! If I couldn't, it was okay because it was great interaction practice.

Fast forward to my present-day life, and we can see the impact this early experience had on me. I've never been afraid to talk to people, go to an event where I knew no one, or try new things. My experience at the Frankfurt Book Fair is one of those memories that will stay with me for the rest of my life, and it is one of the moments that helped shape who I am.

Working at the book fair gave me an early glimpse of what I would later discover to be the Get Stuff Done Factor, or GSD Factor for short. That nine-year old girl learned what it meant to be confident and comfortable in her own skin and how to leverage that confidence to connect with people. I couldn't put a name to it then, but I know now that this trip helped shape my assertiveness, dedication, and my voice. I tip my hat to my dad and thank him for those skill sets that he taught me at such a young age.

ACTIVITY

What gifts do you have?

_____

_____

_____

_____

How can you use those gifts to connect with people?

_____

_____

_____

_____

A SPACE TO DREAM BIG . . .

A SPACE TO DREAM BIG . . .

1

YOUR TRUE AUTHENTIC SELF

You are a unicorn. This is one of the fundamental points to remember when we start to think about what the GSD Factor is. What does this mean? Why a unicorn?

I'm a mom to two great kids, and my husband and I are always looking for books and tools that can help them and us as we navigate parenting in this day and age. One of our favorite tools is called Slumberkins, an organization dedicated to helping families raise caring, confident, and resilient children through affirmations, stories, and creature characters. Slumberkins have developed these amazing characters and turned them into stuffed animals with beautifully-written stories meant to encourage children's emotional growth. Their story of the unicorn is one that shows tiny humans the power of authenticity, and it promotes this alongside bravery and friendship. The story's protagonist is the unicorn, who is unique and authentic but wants to fit in so badly with her new friends, the zebras. Throughout the story, she changes her look and the way she acts in a desperate attempt to conform to her peers. She misses the fact that she is losing herself in the process. She doesn't realize that what makes her unique is tied to her identity. It's her true, authentic self. This story is a creative way to teach kids confidence and self-acceptance, but the lesson is universal across all ages. The first GSD Factor attribute of being confident is directly related to this idea of the unicorn and embracing authenticity. Being confident and assertive about who you are and your beliefs is the fuel that propels one to action. GSDers celebrate uniqueness because we understand that differences cultivate stronger teams, families, and organizations. Diversity creates an atmosphere for endless possibilities, so being a unicorn–distinct, authentic, irreplicable–is an asset and a tell-tale sign of a person who gets stuff done.

So many times, we find ourselves conforming to those around us. We change our look because that's what the celebrities and social media tell us to do. We change how we speak and what we say because it's what everyone else is doing or has done. We make ourselves smaller, so we can blend with the crowd. How much more interesting would life be if instead of changing our looks, personalities, and voices to fit in, we amplified the unique aspects of ourselves to enhance and enrich those around us? If we embraced being the unicorn? What if we used our peculiarities to tell a different story, a unicorn story, a GSD Factor story? Sure, our voice can still be heard in a choir, but when we step forward, into the spotlight, looking, sounding, and acting a little differently, our voice is not only heard but remembered.

Being a unicorn matters in your personal life too. When my daughter was in the first grade, she was assigned one of her first presentations for which she had to make a creative project and prepare a speech about her culture. The same way my father once helped me prepare for my presentations at the Frankfurt Book Fair, my husband and I worked with her, preparing, planning, selecting the creative elements she wanted to display and then the talking points of her speech. We knew it was going to be different from most kids' presentations, but she was excited. She practiced and even sent a video to all the family for the sneak peek. It turned out, though, that she ended up being one of the last kids to present in a class of twenty. As each of her classmates took their turns, my daughter found herself being self-conscious about the fact that everyone else's presentations sounded the same. She was embarrassed that hers was different, and then she started getting scared. She so desperately wanted to fit in with the rest of her classmates.

When she stood up, she changed her entire speech and made it conform to what everyone else had done. She thought it would make her feel good afterwards, but instead she was sad. She got in the car at pickup and started crying, fully aware that she had acted like a zebra and not like the unicorn that she is. At that moment she felt what it's like not to be true to yourself, not to walk in the unicorn or GSD Factor way.

Here's what's most impressive about my daughter's experience. She knew that she had not lived up to her uniqueness, so she decided to correct her errors. The next day, she let her teacher know that she was not content with her presentation. She told the teacher that she had practiced the presentation differently, and she asked if she could redo it at the end of class, if time permitted. Thankfully, there was extra time, and the teacher allowed my little unicorn to present. And present she did! She came home beaming with pride and excitement, not just because of the warm reception from both the teacher and her classmates after she presented, but because of the feeling of accomplishment and peace she got from being authentic. She shed those zebra stripes.

The question I have for you is this: Are you a unicorn or are you a zebra? Being a unicorn embodies the GSD Factor and builds that muscle of confidence each time you choose to stand boldly in your true, authentic self. Being confident becomes much easier when you are consistently embracing all of the differences and unique qualities that make you who you are. It's simple. The more you show up as your true self, the more assertive you can be in challenging and difficult situations.

Be confident in who you are, and don't diminish yourself to make others comfortable. This is your life, and the more you embrace your uniqueness, the more empowered you will feel and become. That's when you can really start to get stuff done!

ACTIVITY

Set a timer for 60 seconds and write all the things you like about yourself.

_____

_____

_____

_____

Set another timer for 60 seconds and write all the things you dislike about yourself.

_____

_____

_____

_____

Which list is longer? _____

Are the things you don't like about yourself flaws or uniqueness? It's important to distinguish between the two. Have you been viewing your uniqueness as a disadvantage/flaw? Use the space below to reflect:

_____

_____

_____

_____

The things we like, dislike, and consider different about ourselves contribute to who we are as a whole. Acknowledging those things and either deciding to accept, capitalize or change them are all parts of embracing your true, authentic self. Look at your lists again. First, really consider whether your dislikes are actually flaws or just unique traits.

Use the chart below to write out the actual flaws, and in the column across from it, write the opposite of the flaw.

FLAW	OPPOSITE

Consider ways that you can evolve or improve upon the things you wrote in both columns and the ways that these traits make you unique. List at least three ways you can use your "uniqueness" to your advantage.

_____

_____

_____

_____

_____

_____

_____

_____

_____

_____

_____

A SPACE TO DREAM BIG . . .

⌐⅃

USE YOUR VOICE

There are lots of ways we can use our voices. My sister and I were both a part of the traveling swim team. Each year, the swim team would have fundraisers to help cover the team's expenses. Depending on the time of year, our campaign could have been frozen pizzas, frozen cookie dough, or wrapping paper. My sister and I were a team, and we were good! If we entered a fundraising competition, the athleticism in us had to make it a competition. We would win hands down. Our dad would sit down with us and plan our goals, daily targets, and how many houses/families we needed to talk to as we were about to hit the streets! After our planning sessions, we would role play and practice. Of course, being the oldest, I was tasked with handling most of the "No" or "Thanks, but no thanks" responses, while my sister handled most of the "Yes" customers.

Just like the Frankfurt Book Fair, Dad coached us on how to respond in every situation. When we would make a sale, we would leave the new customer with the next steps for their order, including details about when we would deliver. We even wrote out individual thank you notes for each donor. Yes! My sister was as young as eight, and I was twelve! Our dad would drop us off at one end of the subdivision and tell us where he expected us to be in the neighborhood by a certain time. The Bleymaier sisters were a force to be reckoned with!

Another major lesson about using our voice that I reflect on the most when remembering these fundraisers is how Dad made sure that we told our potential donors *why* we were raising money and what made it relevant to us. The reason is what makes the emotional connection for someone. Perhaps your school raises money for your band or dance troupe. Perhaps they raise money for the American Heart Association. You never know who you are talking to. Maybe the person was in a band when they were younger, or they themselves have a heart problem that your fundraiser is trying to bring awareness to. Whatever it may be, making that emotional connection makes it personal.

ACTIVITY

Has there been a time in your life where you wish your voice had been your strongest weapon?

_____

_____

_____

_____

_____

_____

_____

_____

_____

_____

A SPACE TO DREAM BIG . . .

A SPACE TO DREAM BIG . . .

PASSION AND DEDICATION

Everything up until this point has been about who you are and how you show up in the world. We've discussed the importance of being confident and brave; embracing your true, authentic self; and using your voice to empower yourself and others. All of these qualities play an important part in living the GSD Factor life. Now let's talk about passion and dedication and how they fit into this puzzle. What's the difference between passion and dedication?

Passion is the GSD Factor attribute that equates to the fire in your belly to get stuff done. It's the love of something so deep that you can't imagine not doing it. If asked to sacrifice something for your passion, there is zero hesitation. It comes to you as natural as breathing. You go to sleep thinking about it. You dream about it, and in the morning, you have fresh ideas about it. Your passion does not feel like work to you. No matter how tough life is, you show up. You dig deep for it. You are striving to improve it, to be the best you can be.

Dedication is the GSD Factor attribute that serves as the grit and the stamina driving your passion to the point of excellence and greatness. It's the drive in your life that says one sport, one after-school activity or one passion is not enough. It's the drive that says studying and training on the bare minimum is settling. It's the attitude that consistently goes above and beyond, arrives early and stays late, even on weekends. It's also the wisdom to know when to rest and recharge.

ACTIVITY

Let's practice introducing ourselves. Stand in front of a mirror and be sure to maintain eye contact, smile, and stretch out your right hand. Give a strong firm shake to the air. While doing this, say the following:

Hi my name is _____. Nice to meet you.

You can also practice other conversation starters:

I'm in the _____ grade and attend _____ school.

My favorite subject in school is _____.

Outside of school I'm interested in _____

_____

_____   _____

_____.

When I grow up I want to be a _____

_____

_____

A SPACE TO DREAM BIG . . .

A SPACE TO DREAM BIG . . .

ACTION PLAN

HOW TO BE CONFIDENT

Be confident or be bold. The sentence is simple, but the concept is rather complex. This first, and possibly most important GSD Factor attribute is composed of three smaller keys: Knowing and embracing your true authentic self, using your voice, and finding your passion and dedication.

With teenagers and adults who want to improve their confidence and assertiveness, I tend to recommend role play, coaching, or even acting classes. When faced with a difficult situation or conversation, role-playing can be an effective way to prepare for every scenario. My mom and dad did it with me all throughout my life, and it has worked. You can do this alone or with your mentor, friends, or family members. Whatever the circumstance, role-playing allows you to practice the tone, volume, and authority of your voice.

Here are three steps for role-playing:

1. Think about the situation or conversation, and write out all of the possible scenarios that could develop, including the opposing side of things. This will give you an opportunity to have a response ready for a variety of comments. You can't predict the future, but this will bolster your confidence as you prepare for the conversation. You won't feel like you're going into the situation blind.

2. Get with a mentor or friend and talk through every scenario that you listed. It is helpful to work with a teammate because you will have real-time feedback on the quality and effectiveness of your arguments and comments.

3. In addition to practicing with a mentor or friend, it is also helpful to practice in the mirror. This will make you aware of your body language and facial expressions. If you're confident in how you look, you'll be more confident in what you are saying. You would be surprised how helpful this can be.

ACTIVITY

We just practiced introducing ourselves in the mirror. Now let's reflect on the power of body language and facial expressions:

Stand in front of a mirror and observe your body language and facial expressions. What do you notice? How does your body language impact your confidence? What does your body language communicate? Do you see your full self reflected?
   Write about the importance of confident, non-verbal communication and how practicing in front of a mirror can improve your overall assertiveness.

_____

_____

_____

_____

_____

_____

Flip back to any of the activities throughout this chapter and read your answers out loud confidently. Try different expressions, stances, postures. Find the best for you and practice.

A Mantra for Being Confident

I know who I am.

I am confident.

I am bold.

I embrace my true, authentic self.

I do not apologize for being me.

I use my voice for myself.

I use my voice for others.

I am passionate.

I am dedicated.

See me.

Hear me.

Know me.

I know who I am.

A SPACE TO DREAM BIG . . .

ATTRIBUTE TWO

BE INQUISITIVE

Being inquisitive means asking "why" to investigate, grow our own knowledge, and learn something from everything.

"

The greatest thing about tomorrow is, I will be better than I am today...There is no such thing as a setback. The lessons I learned today I will apply tomorrow, and I will be better.

– TIGER WOODS

"

ACTIVITY

List some of your favorite ways of learning new things.

_____

_____

_____

_____

_____

_____

_____

_____

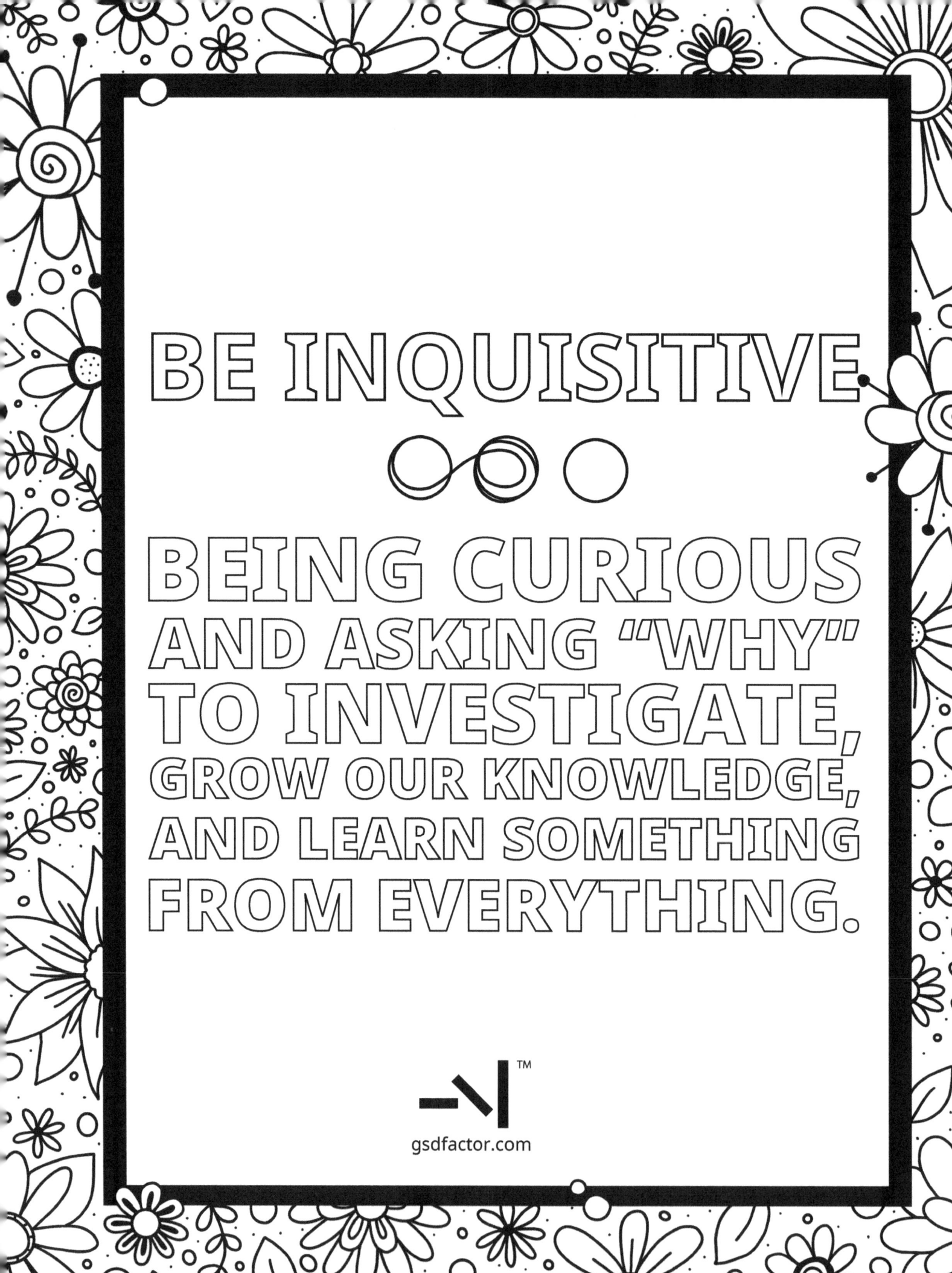

BE INQUISITIVE

BEING CURIOUS AND ASKING "WHY" TO INVESTIGATE, GROW OUR KNOWLEDGE, AND LEARN SOMETHING FROM EVERYTHING.

gsdfactor.com

ALWAYS LEARN SOMETHING

There aren't many things that I know to be absolutes in this world. However, I do know at least one absolute fact: no one person knows everything. Even though there may not be one source to reference for all of life's questions, I'm a firm believer that you can learn something from every experience, whether it's your own experience or something you hear along the way that can make an impact. There are many places from where we can learn things: TikTok, podcasts, books. Overall, great learning can be gleaned by observing others.

So, how do we learn something from every experience? One of the things I like to do after an experience is facilitate my own debrief, a review of sorts. I ask questions of others and of myself. For example, I might ask:

- Did I accomplish what I set out to do?

- What could I have done better or worse?

- How could I have responded differently?

- Did I listen?

- Did I hear?

- Did my point of view come across?

ACTIVITY

What types of questions do you ask yourself after experiencing something positive?

_____

_____

_____

_____

What types of questions do you ask yourself after experiencing something negative?

_____

_____

_____

_____

In addition to recognizing that there is a learning opportunity in every situation, life has also allowed me to develop the ability to determine whether a lesson is one that will teach future-me what TO DO or what NOT TO DO. I have had lots of mentors and heroes from whom I have learned both sides of this equation. I believe we can look to those in our lives or from a distance and ask, "What can I learn from you, so that I don't have to live it?"

Perhaps throughout your life you have had relationships that were chosen for you or that you encountered that weren't always the best. Maybe they came with a lot of toxic or negative interactions. Within each of these moments you are faced with two choices: you could be bitter or angry because you have to engage with those people, or you could choose to look at their lives or choices from a different view point.

The dynamic between my late father and me was a great example of this type of interaction. My father and I didn't always have the best father-daughter relationship. It was messy. It was complicated. We certainly had some precious memories that I will treasure, but it wasn't an easy relationship. We both had to work hard to make the relationship work. At times, we took breaks from it, and that's okay. In our own ways, we were both broken people, and that didn't always bring out the best in us. However, towards the latter years of my dad's life, we were able to get really honest. In one of these moments of truth, I said to him, "I love you. I will honor you as my father because that's what our faith calls for. You will always be my dad, but there are times, in my life, when you have taught me more of what not to do than what to do."

These words, as honest as they were, were not the easiest to say, and they weren't the easiest for him to hear. However, in his last letter to me before he died, he acknowledged them. He was grateful for the reconciliation we had worked so hard for. He acknowledged that my words were true and that he was sorry he couldn't have done better. He asked that I continue to live my life and grow my family but that I would not forget him; that I share stories with my kids about their Papa Teddy; and that I be sure to share not only the good lessons, but also the lessons he wished he had learned earlier.

That moment of acknowledging that someone in your life, be it a family member, teacher, friend or coach, is actually teaching you what not to do can be extremely impactful. That's when you have to confront the tough, unblocked, unfiltered realities of life. The fullness of those lessons makes a much greater impact on our lives than we may realize. I think, in this society, we just expect that we are going to be taught what to do, how to do it, and get all the steps to success explicitly. It's less popular to look at a situation and ask, "What did I learn not to do?"

My challenge to you is this. Look back on some of your interactions, relationships, or connections, recent or otherwise, and ask yourself, "What did I learn? Did I learn what to do or what not to do?" Ask yourself these questions from a place of gratitude, and it will completely transform your outlook on the past and present. Learning from the past opens up opportunities for growing in your future. This newfound inquisitiveness will allow you a level of grace and forgiveness, should you want it, that will give you wings of freedom. You won't regret past decisions or mistakes because you will realize that you are still able to learn from those things, and these lessons will help you get stuff done.

That's where this GSD Factor mindset of learning something from every experience originates. I challenge your ego to take a seat. Listen to those around you when you enter a room. What can you learn from them? You can learn SOMETHING from everyone.

ACTIVITY

Think of a person who impacts your life, positively or negatively.

_____

_____

What has that person taught you to do?

_____

_____

_____

What has that person taught you not to do?

_____

_____

_____

A SPACE TO DREAM BIG . . .

A SPACE TO DREAM BIG . . .

GSD FACTOR SQUAD

Friends, you all have both the gift and possible curse of youth. The gift is that when you're as young as you are, you're a clean slate. A world of experiences is ahead of you and the possibilities for your future can be endless. The curse of youth though, is that you don't yet have the experience or foresight to move fully independently yet. To be honest, many adults don't have that either, but it's magnified for you simply because of the number of years you've been on the planet. I have a solution for that.

In my book, I speak of the need for all GSDers to have a group of people who serve as advisors and helpers in different areas of their lives, both professionally and personally. I call these groups of people the GSD Insiders Board and the GSD Clan. A GSDer's Board and Clan provide support and guidance in many areas of the GSDer's life, from mental and physical health to finances and spirituality. Though you are young and may or may not have a professional life yet, you too can benefit from having groups of people like this. You might call them your "squad."

ACTIVITY

Before reading any further, make a list of who you consider to be part of your squad?

_____

_____

_____

_____

_____

_____

_____

You are the leader of your own GSD Factor Squad. No ifs, ands, or buts on this one. You, and only you alone, can fulfill this role and its responsibilities. As we embark on building your GSD Factor Squad, know that communicating to your individual Squad members that you consider them to be part of your Squad is key. Additionally, it's important, especially if it's a friend or family member, to ask them if they are willing to be part of your GSD Factor Squad. You are going to reach out to them. Look to them for guidance and feedback. Identifying, naming, communicating, and getting buy-in from your GSD Factor Squad will ensure your success as you are on this GSD Factor transformation.

If you were able to name a number of people, that's great! Raised as a Liverpool Football Club fan, I heard "You'll Never Walk Alone" played and sung throughout our house and many family gatherings. The words ring so true: "Walk on, walk on. With hope in your heart. And you'll never walk alone." This journey called life was never meant for us to be alone or do it alone. As we grow up, we experience different, sometimes difficult things that may make us *feel* alone, but it is important to believe and understand that, even then, we are never alone. Even in a world that has families separated by thousands of miles and the familial generational unit is less common, we still look to our families, those to whom we've been born and those that we have chosen. Iron sharpens iron. We can support one another. We know that we can learn from one another. We watch each other.

If you named one or two people, that's amazing too! Your journey so far may have looked less crowded than others', but at the end of the day, you have at least one person that has helped or is helping you along the way. Fighter pilots don't just have a co-pilot, they have a wingman. That wingman is there to maintain formation no matter if it's in front, behind, or to the side. They are constantly watching out for the main fighter pilot and running interference if necessary.

Now that you have thought about your current squad, think about the types of roles each member plays in your life. There are a lot of different roles and responsibilities that Squad members can take. Here are different types that you can consider:

- Your Spiritual member

- Your Mental Health member

- Your Self-Care member

- Your Physical member

- Your Hero member

- Your Dreamer member

- Your Execution member

- Your Cheerleader member

You may have several people that fulfill multiple roles, but each role brings a distinct value to your life. Your GSD Factor Squad should grow and evolve with you as you are ever growing and evolving. We humans must continue to grow, learn, be stretched, and be challenged. Your GSD Factor Squad should do the same, and if it's not, then friend, it's time to evaluate and make sure your members are meeting you where you are on your journey.

At your age, you'll probably find that most of your Squad will probably be your friends and members of your family. However, friends and family members are not the only people you can look toward to be a part of your Squad. As a matter of fact, you'll quickly find that people from all aspects of your life can fill these roles.

YOUR SPIRITUAL SQUAD MEMBER

My spiritual side recommends having a spiritual member. Perhaps it's a priest or pastor, or if you don't have a formal faith practice, then you can still seek out spiritual guides. Being in alignment with a higher power and ensuring you are nurturing your soul are foundational cornerstones for your life.

MENTAL HEALTH SQUAD MEMBER

Be sure to think about your soul, spirit, mind, and body and whether they are fully represented in your GSD Factor Squad. We have touched a little bit on soul and even spirit, but the mind is just as important. You need that mental health Squad member. It could be a therapist, school counselor, personal coach, or even all of the above.

YOUR SELF-CARE SQUAD MEMBER

Similar to the mental health Squad member is the self-care Squad member who is equally as important. Think of what the flight attendants tell plane travelers as they are reciting the safety procedures. They always say, "Please put on your mask before helping others." We should think of self-care in the same way. Be sure your self-care centers around being loving, present, and extending grace and mercy to yourself first. It helps to have someone in your life who will remind you of that.

YOUR PHYSICAL SQUAD MEMBER

Next is your physical Squad member. This is a great time to share an example of Squad members who serve in more than one capacity. Maybe you participate in sports such as soccer, basketball, dance, cheerleading, softball, or karate. Any of your teammates can be considered one of your mental health squad members *and* one of your physical squad members. Your coach is your physical member, but given there are therapeutic benefits to being active and being part of a team, they can also double up as one of your mental health squad members. Your physical member encourages you to get your body moving in some way. Even if you don't participate in sports, it's just as important to get moving such as walking outside, embracing nature and the energy that comes from that. There is scientific evidence that supports that physical exercise is beneficial to our bodies, minds, and emotions, so do not neglect this member!

YOUR HERO SQUAD MEMBER

The hero Squad member is who you aspire to be like. It could be someone you know or even someone you don't know at all. It could be someone that is alive or has passed. Consider someone in your community, your parents, teachers, athletes or artists. Whoever your hero is, they should inspire you to be the best version of yourself. They should be someone you can look to when your journey becomes difficult and you need that extra push to keep showing up.

YOUR DREAMER SQUAD MEMBERS

Now let's talk about the dreamer or the visionary Squad member. If you struggle to dream or cast a vision for yourself, find that person that will be your dreamer and your visionary. We can get so caught in the daily rhythm of life that we forget to dream, forget to think about the horizon and possibilities. When we dream, it unlocks that hope of possibility. It unlocks creativity. It unlocks what *could* be. Think about someone that inspires you, maybe they are a friend or someone famous you have read about or watched, perhaps they have accomplished things that you want to accomplish. Your dreamer Squad member is the person who will get you to think and see your life in ways that you cannot or struggle to imagine.

YOUR EXECUTION SQUAD MEMBERS

With any dream or vision, you also need a plan to execute. This is where your execution Squad member comes in. Just think, you know where you are today and you know where you want to go, but do you have a roadmap or plan to get there? You need the map with the milestones that need to be hit in order to achieve. This person is your execution master. They will guide you, remind you of what needs to be done to reach that dream or vision in the timeline or date you set for yourself, and assist you in completing these goals and projects. Consider your guidance counselor, skills coach, study buddy, or the captain of your team–whomever you call when you need to get stuff done. As with all of the GSD Factor Squad positions, this execution member will really be unique to your life and needs. Whoever it is, this person helps you get stuff done in the most literal sense.

YOUR CHEERLEADER SQUAD MEMBER

Many times, people associate their encouragement or cheerleader with their execution master, but I would argue you don't necessarily want them to be the same person. Your cheerleader is the person who allows you to express your feelings, hears your cries and screams. Your cheerleader helps pick you back up, dusts you off, and reminds you of your dreams. Ideally, everybody in your Squad will be cheering you on and encouraging in some way, but it's good to know that you have a few people that you can go to and always get support and motivation.

ACTIVITY

Now that you know the GSD Factor Squad roles, fill in the people in your life who serve as your members.

My Spiritual member is _____

My Mental Health member is _____

My Self-Care member is _____

My Physical member is _____

My Hero member is _____

My Dreamer member is _____

My Execution member is _____

My Cheerleader member is _____

This GSD Factor Squad is important because it's imperative to get the input of others. This second GSD Factor attribute is based on being inquisitive–being curious, asking questions, soliciting the knowledge and wisdom of others. Success does not come to people in isolation because no one can obtain success strictly off of their own skills or merit. Living the GSD Factor life means being fully aware that you do not know everything, nor are you the best at everything. The healthy GSDer knows that and is not hesitant to tap their Squad members on the shoulder for help when necessary.

Remember that some of your GSD Factor Squad members may serve in a couple of member roles. For example, your self-care member might also be your physical member, or your dreamer is also your cheerleader. That's fine. This is your GSD Factor Squad. You get to build and pull together those squad members for you. And do not forget that what your GSD Factor Squad looks like today may not be the GSD Factor Squad you need tomorrow. As you continue to grow in your GSD Factor transformation, so will your Squad.

ACTIVITY

Step 1: Use the chart below to list all your strengths and weaknesses.

Step 2: Next to your strengths, fill in the name of someone you know who excels in this area as well.

Step 3: Next to your weaknesses, fill in the name of someone you know who excels in this area.

STRENGTH	NAME	WEAKNESS	NAME

Now, consider this: Could any of those people be members of your GSD Factor Squad?

Maybe those people are already unofficially serving in that role in your life. Whether they are or not, consider having a conversation with them explaining that you'd like to lean on them for support in that area.

A SPACE TO DREAM BIG . . .

ACTION PLAN

HOW TO BE INQUISITIVE

The key to being inquisitive is understanding that we are always learning. Your goal is to always be curious and to be a student of life. Being inquisitive gives you the humble awareness that you are not the smartest person in the room, but the knowledge to know how to mobilize the right team of people to ensure that you are open to the fullness of life. Look at life with a glass half-full approach. Search for lessons in what to do and what not to do. As lifelong learners, it is imperative to be surrounded by the right people. Accountability makes everyone better. It is also important to note that the people we surround ourselves with may change as we grow and evolve as humans and this is okay.

A Mantra for Being Inquisitive

I am curious.

I am inquisitive.

I watch.

I listen.

I learn from everything.

I learn from everyone.

I am smart.

I am humble.

I am happy.

Positive energy surrounds me.

I am never alone.

I am always learning.

I will always have all that I need.

A SPACE TO DREAM BIG . . .

A SPACE TO DREAM BIG . . .

A SPACE TO DREAM BIG . . .

ATTRIBUTE THREE

BE IMAGINATIVE

Being imaginative means dreaming big.
It means saying yes to the seemingly impossible and
pushing yourself beyond even your own imagination.

> They said I can't live my dreams.
> I ignored them.
>
> – TAYLOR SWIFT

ACTIVITY

If there were no obstacles in your way, who would you be?

_____

_____

_____

_____

_____

_____

_____

_____

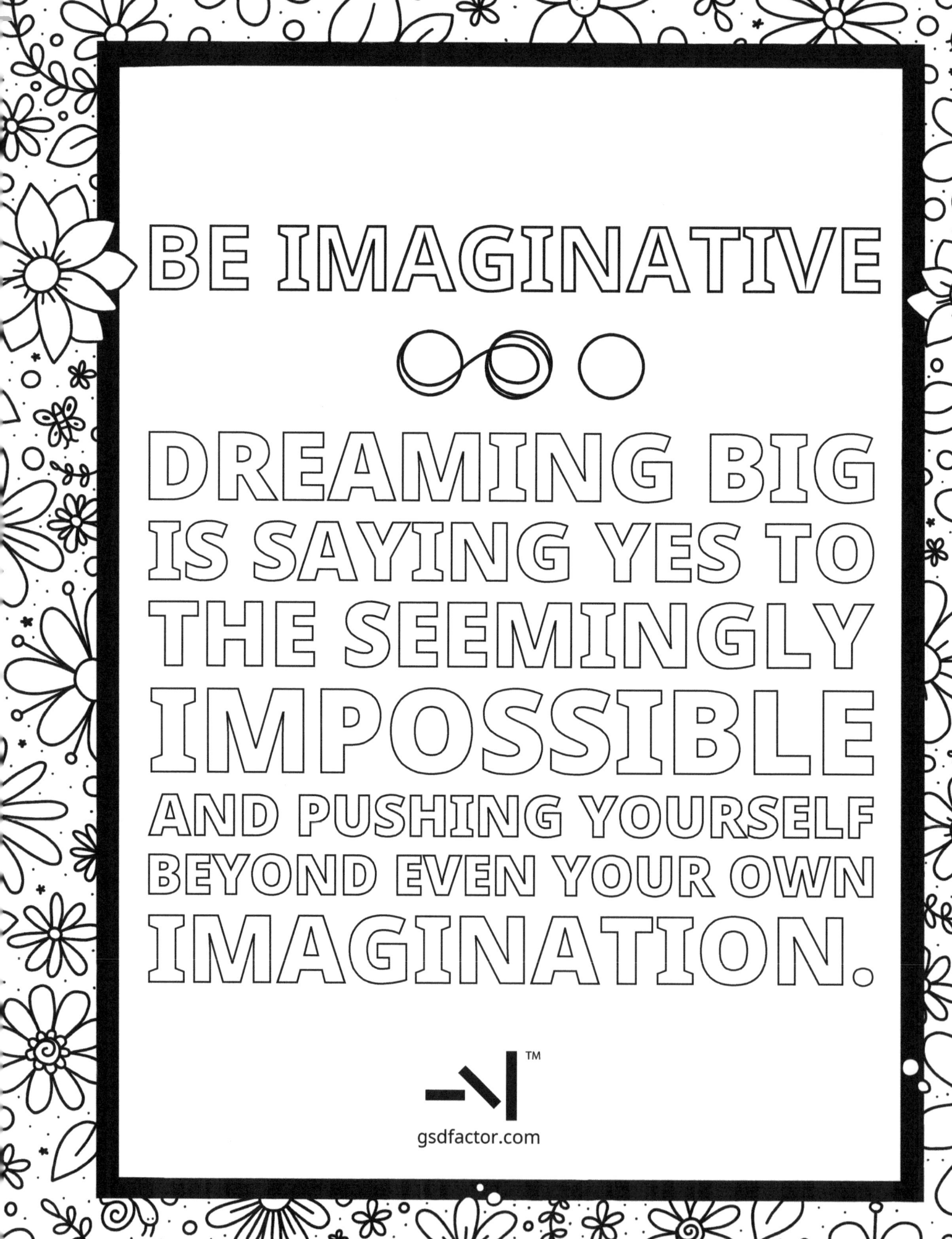

BE IMAGINATIVE

DREAMING BIG IS SAYING YES TO THE SEEMINGLY IMPOSSIBLE AND PUSHING YOURSELF BEYOND EVEN YOUR OWN IMAGINATION.

gsdfactor.com

DREAM BIG

My team hears it. My clients hear it. My kids hear it. Imagination and dreams go hand in hand. For the first sixteen years of my life, my dream was dancing, but after facing sickness and injury, I realized that dreams could change. The injuries I incurred necessitated the change, but the experience just shed light on dreams that were always there–dreams of entrepreneurship, mentoring, and organizational leadership. I had been operating in those dreams all my life, but because dance was my number one priority, those other dreams just moved to the back burner. The third GSD Factor attribute–being imaginative–is all about keeping that dream-big muscle active and recognizing all the possibilities of your back-burner dreams.

As someone who is highly organized, follows rules, and has everything planned out, my ability to dream had to evolve. My difficulty came in allowing myself to dream freely, to resist the urge to be practical and logistical and just let my imagination run wild. Sometimes, I have to force myself to dream, but thankfully, I have people who remind me to do so. I'm now operating fully in entrepreneurship and mentorship, so my dreams look different. They still involve a great deal of imagination, but now my dreams are all about being open to the opportunities that become available to me and knowing how to be in the moment.

Perhaps that's why I've gotten good at helping people dream big for themselves and their organizations. I was at a hockey game with my husband, hanging out at our regular spot in the arena, and this group of fellow hockey fans joined us. We immediately hit it off and started talking about careers, jobs, and companies. There was one gentleman who commented that he didn't make a lot of money, but that his life circumstances really needed him to. I kept asking questions. I asked him about his vision, his ideal job, his ideal role, his ideal company. I was forcing him to do some self-reflection. He and I kept talking throughout the evening as he was seeking clarity and diving deeper and deeper with each question.

Through the course of questions and conversations, he was starting to think about things differently. What started as questions turned into discovery and ultimately landed us on what I call his "Dream Big" for himself. He said he had never thought about his skill sets in the way we were talking about them then, never thought about applying them differently to get a different outcome. Those questions began to plant seeds–seeds of hope, seeds of dreams, seeds of what could be. Some months later, he reached out to let me know that our one conversation ignited something in him that he had forgotten about. He was able to transform himself and find a job that was in more alignment with what he wanted and is now making two to three times more than what he was previously making. Our conversation (more like me listening and asking questions) over a meal and hockey completely changed his life's direction.

When I think about the evolution of my dreams, I can see now that what I saw as a hindrance to my dreams–the way I leaned toward practicality and logic–could actually be an asset, as long as there is balance between logic and imagination. A major part of being imaginative and dreaming big is to figure out how to transform those dreams into reality. The best way to do that is to just allow yourself to dream. Let your imagination roam freely, but then access your practical mind and the ways to make the impossible happen.

How do you access your practical mind to make the impossible happen? That's where you have to do a little work, friends. Dreaming big is great, but until you put a plan together, it's just a dream. You might have to get on Google and look for people who have done similar things. Do some research. Your dream may seem impossible, but you'd be surprised how much more attainable it will become once you start discovering other people who have achieved similar feats. Seeing these other people's successes and even their failures can be just the motivation and inspiration you need to make your dreams happen. It's going to take some effort, but that's how we get stuff done.

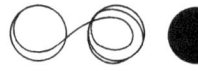

ACTIVITY

Grab three note cards or sticky notes, and write down one big dream or ambition on each note card/sticky note.

Don't think about how big or impossible the dream seems. Just write it down and place them around your room, locker, or other personal space that you see every day. Look over them. Read them out loud. Dream about them. You are manifesting them, which means you are calling them to happen.

A SPACE TO DREAM BIG . . .

A SPACE TO DREAM BIG . . .

7

NEVER BE SATISFIED

My grandfather General Joseph S. Bleymaier, or Papa Joe as we called him, was a major general in the United States Air Force who fought in World War II and led Air Force support efforts for NASA in the race to the moon and the Titan rocket program. He was brilliant, a literal rocket scientist. Because of my grandfather's history with NASA and the Space Program, I've always been fascinated and inspired by the Space Race of the sixties. As the country prepared for the challenge, President John F. Kennedy addressed the nation before the space efforts began back in September 1962. He famously said, "We choose to go to the Moon in this decade and do the other things, not because they are easy, but because they are hard." President Kennedy's words are at the crux of the GSD Factor attribute of being imaginative, and they coincide with the next sub attribute–never be satisfied.

We've talked about being imaginative as it relates to dreaming big, and never being satisfied is the next step to maximizing your imagination's potential. The United States' dedication to winning the Space Race is a great example of this type of ideology because of all the seemingly insurmountable odds that our space program was facing at the time. Many said it couldn't be done. At the time, our space program was behind, very behind. The money wasn't there. The infrastructure wasn't there. We didn't have the right technology.

This wasn't a small project. It was putting a man on the moon and returning him back to Earth safely, which was a feat no one had done, and especially not with a program that was behind the technological curve. For example, in order to complete interstellar orbits, one of the first things we needed was satellites, and the first working satellite, Sputnik, was not created by the U.S., but by the Soviet Union. We basically started the race from behind. To add insult to injury, President John F. Kennedy addressed the nation with this challenge, "But if I were to say, my fellow citizens, that we shall send to the moon… and do all this, and do it right, and do it first before this decade is out–then we must be bold."

Talk about pressure! Think of how daunting a task that already was, but adding a timeline of fewer than eight years made it especially impossible. Still, with the backing of our president, our country and our citizens said yes. We embodied boldness. We innovated. We DREAMED BIG.

There were many set-backs, but the tide eventually turned in our favor with the Americans being the first to send a crew into space to orbit the moon. We didn't stop there though. We weren't satisfied with just orbiting the moon. We had to land there, and in July of 1969, with less than six months left in the decade, we did. That moment is memorialized by Neil Armstrong's famous quote, "That's one small step for a man, one giant leap for mankind."

As you can tell, I really fan-girl out on this story. If you're wondering why the space program is near and dear to my heart, it's because there are lots of connections between the moon landing and my career in the technology industry and GSD Factor. You could say it runs in my blood. The GSD Factor didn't start with me; it flows through my DNA, and it came from my grandfather. It was his contribution to and involvement with the space program that makes it a little more special to me. He was a part of the people who weren't satisfied with being second best. My grandfather said yes to the president. He said yes to his country by helping to train the astronauts who would eventually work on some of these special projects during this pivotal time in our country's technological history. He dreamed big. Today, he has an award in the Smithsonian, and his many decorations include the Legion of Merit and the Air Medal with oak leaf cluster.

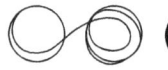

ACTIVITY

Name someone who dreamed beyond what had already been done to achieve something new?

_____

_____

_____

_____

_____

The drive of never being satisfied and never settling embodied my grandfather's life and mission and he passed this to me as one of the key attributes of the GSD Factor Life. I've also faced times in my professional career that had challenges similar to those that my grandfather had to face during the space race. One of those times came fairly recently in March 2020 right as the United States implemented the first mandatory shutdown of the country. The Covid-19 pandemic was probably one of the most uncertain health crises of my lifetime, and because I had just been hired as the new head of technology for an insurance company, my team and I were now being asked to make drastic technological changes in the face of uncertainty and navigating how we would be able to interact with our customers. The short version of our task was that we needed to rebuild, rethink, and re-engineer what technology would look like to serve the insurance community in the midst of a pandemic. Oh, yeah, and we had to do it in six months!

For the next several months, my team and I worked hundred-hour work weeks to build technology that would allow us to complete insurance quotes for clients and go through the enrollment process electronically which had historically been done in person. The technology was so innovative and game-changing that we started garnering the attention of our competitors, government agencies, and eventually buyers. Eventually, our technology stack was the catalyst that led to the company being bought in December of that same year. For me, that whole experience, though exhausting, further solidified the never-be-satisfied genes I inherited from my grandfather.

I know that I come from ancestors on both sides of my family that embraced and amplified innovation, drive, dreaming big, and never being satisfied, but I believe that this lives within each of us. Whether your ancestral history has examples of this for you to follow or not, you are responsible for your history, *your story*, the story that your lineage will speak about. Ask yourself, "What should I never be satisfied about?" Whatever it is, try saying yes, because in the words of famed American author and activist, Glennon Doyle, "We can do hard things."

So don't avoid those difficulties or challenges. Tackle them head on with your imagination and that spirit of never being satisfied. Who knows? You may surprise yourself and impact history just like my grandfather and the ingenious men and women he worked with during the Space Race.

ACTIVITY

Answer the following questions about yourself:

What situation do you find yourself in that you are not satisfied with?

_____

_____

_____

_____

Is there something you have observed in your community that stirs an excitement in your belly that makes you want to take action?

_____

_____

_____

_____

A SPACE TO DREAM BIG . . .

A SPACE TO DREAM BIG . . .

PROBLEMS LEAD TO SOLUTIONS

Everyone has problems. People have problems getting along with co-workers, problems saving money, problems maintaining healthy lifestyles. The list goes on.

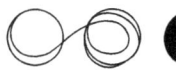

ACTIVITY

Give yourself ten seconds and name three problems (big or small) that you have.

_____

_____

_____

_____

_____

_____

Everyone also *sees* problems. These are problems that are noticeable to everyone but can't necessarily be changed on an individual level. For example, we see problems with the environment, problems with the education system, problems in politics, even problems we see with our friends, family members, or co-workers.

ACTIVITY

Give yourself ten seconds and name three problems that you've seen but can't change on your own.

_____

_____

_____

_____

_____

_____

_____

_____

Now, problems are unavoidable. Whether at home, at work, among family, or among friends, we all face them. I believe, though, that the way we approach problems separates us into two types of people: problem-pointers and problem-solvers.

There is a great book by Kirk A. Weisler called, *The Dog Poop Initiative*, which provides a great lesson into problem-pointers and problem-solvers. The book's purpose is to teach readers how to be proactive citizens who make efforts to better every environment they are in, even when they don't necessarily have to.

Essentially, in *The Dog Poop Initiative*, a dog takes a dump out on a soccer pitch. We won't address the fact that the owner didn't pick it up in the first place, but dog owners, you know who you are; do better. Over the course of a day, there are multiple soccer matches where parents, coaches, referees, and even kids are problem-pointers and even great problem-communicators to anyone that was coming to the pitch. The book goes on about how the pointers consistently and vehemently pointed at the poop. The communicators made sure to warn other people to avoid the poop. Some even complained about the poop. They changed where they played. They changed how they played, but no one tried to solve the problem. The author goes on to say that about 220 people avoided the poop that day, and, in the end, only two actually took action to scoop the poop. That's not even one percent. Seriously?! That's art imitating life, though.

Think about how many times a day you hear someone complain about a problem, and compare that with how many times you actually see or hear about people who take the initiative to fix a problem that is staring right at them? The time and resources spent by the rest of the population pointing it out, complaining, and over-communicating is staggering. What if, as a population and a world, we just moved that needle just a little, even to a full one percent? How different would our world look? How different would companies run?

Being a problem-solver and not a problem-pointer is one of the main fundamentals of living the GSD Factor life. If you find yourself on the solving side of that categorization, then you're probably a person who, as we know I like to say, gets stuff done. Don't get too excited yet, because being that type of person comes with its own set of risks. If you're a natural-born GSDer, then you don't have a problem finding and implementing solutions to problems. You know how to use your imagination to dream big, and when it comes to problem-solving, you understand how important it is to never be satisfied.

However, the real discipline for people who are born with the gift of problem-solving and GSDing comes when it's time to determine what *kind* of solution to use. I'm talking about the MVP here. No, that's not the *most valuable player*. It's the *minimum viable product*. It's a term used in the business world that basically means figuring out what solution you can come up with that works and creates time for you to rest and prepare for a permanent solution. Finding and applying the interim solution rather than immediately beginning work on the long-term solution is a skill that will serve problem-solvers well because it allows you the time to rest and avoid the stress of always diving head-first into long-term solutions. Now, all hope is not lost if you find yourself on the opposite side of the problem-solver/problem-pointer coin. If you're not one of those people who immediately sees solutions, or perhaps you are a problem-pointer, it's okay. We are all works in progress, and you, too, can develop those skills and eventually become a master solutionist.

My high school instructor never gave out tests; he gave "opportunities." What if we thought about problems in the same way? If you think about it, you probably have "opportunities" every day–moments or challenges that, with the right perspective shift, are chances for problem-solving or growth. I have them all the time. Once you realize you have an opportunity, ask yourself if you have a solution. Am I saying that you cannot express frustrations or difficulties? No, you most certainly have a right to your frustrations, and it's healthy for you to express them. However, there is a time and a place for everything, so I do suggest that if you need to vent about something, do it in the appropriate setting, to the appropriate people and in the appropriate manner. Otherwise, you run the risk of being perceived as a complainer, and nobody likes a complainer.

If you're good at identifying problems or opportunities, how do you then turn towards becoming a problem solver? To be an effective problem solver, our mindset and state of being need to be unified and focused on peace. Anxiety is often our first response to problems or conflicts. Oftentimes, anxiety coupled with fear can block our brains from solutioning and finding the answers; this amplifies the fear, causing us to be insecure. We don't want to give power or add fuel to the problem, we want to work the problem. In my experience, I've learned that solutions and answers arise organically from an aligned peaceful state of mind.

For example, have you ever been in a situation that was stressful, and you couldn't think straight? I've experienced this kind of stress a few times, but it was particularly recognizable as we got closer to the deadlines of a number of major projects. I was experiencing solution fatigue, which is exactly what it sounds like. My brain was tired of solving problems, so it would become increasingly more difficult for me to do so. When those times came, I didn't try to push through the fatigue. I would stop working and go for a walk or spend time with my family. Sometimes the most practical solution would be to go take a quick power nap. I love power naps! Those power naps work wonders for my weary brain, and when I wake up, I'm refreshed and ready to get stuff done.

Why is this? For the same reason you need to shut down or restart your phone or computer sometimes, your brain needs to reboot; it needs a rest. When you wake up, you are more likely to be in a peaceful state, and suddenly, ideas start flowing. My recommendation is having something by your bed on which you can capture ideas because as you are sleeping, the brain is recharging. You may wake up with a brilliant idea that you need to record before getting back to sleep. You never know. Finding a state of rest and peace is about groundedness. It's about finding a center.

Each person finds their center in their own way, but you have to come up with a wellness plan and strategy for yourself to be able to get back to your center. If finding that peaceful state of mind is a struggle, I recommend some breathing exercises, meditations or visualizations to aid you in that process. I've often heard that peace is a state of rest and calmness in the soul.

ACTIVITY

Has there ever been a time when getting rest helped you solve a problem?

_____

_____

_____

_____

_____

_____

_____

_____

_____

_____

Once you've found a peaceful mindset, presenting a problem with a solution can become much easier and more systematic. Before you can actually present a solution to a problem, it would be helpful to first identify the size and scope of the problem. To do this effectively, we need more information. We get more information by, first and foremost, listening.

One of the great attributes of a leader is their ability and willingness to listen. Sometimes we problem-solvers are so ready to jump into action that we don't listen and miss important pieces of information. If you can't tell, I'm a problem-solver, and there are many times when I have to remind myself to stop and listen. I exercise this skill on a daily basis with my team and clients. On a personal level, my husband and I have a phrase that we use when we are sharing problems that are going on. We say, "I need you to listen," or "I need you to help me solve this." This came after a few times of us sharing with one another in hopes that the other would just listen, but instead, we jumped to solutioning. This usually caused us to miss the entire point and even propose the wrong solution because we didn't take the time to listen to the problem in its entirety.

Once you have a basic understanding of the problem, the second step is to focus on not being afraid to ask some clarifying questions. Depending on the temperature of the situation, you can ask, "May I ask some clarifying questions? It will help me navigate as I prepare a solution." If the moment is not right, revert back to listening, and come back to that person at a later time to gain the clarity you need. Now that we have our problem, and we are gaining clarity through questions, we can continue to figure out how big our problem is, which will help make our solution more effective.

My daughter gave me a great example of this one day with some homework from her life skills class. Her school counselor used weather as the analogy for assessing problems and how to approach them. The scale she used is brilliant, and I've adapted the same ideologies to the business world.

- Windy = tiny problem, no biggie – Handle on your own.

- Rainy = small problem – Engage with a friend or classmate to solve.

- Stormy = medium problem – Engage with multiple people to solve.

- Tornado = big problem – Get help from a trusted adult to solve.

I think we can all agree that problems and challenges are an inevitable, unavoidable part of life. It would be great if more people took the initiative to be problem-solvers, rather than just problem-pointers, but that's not reality. Actually, being a problem-pointer, in itself, isn't bad. There's value in being able to identify problems. However, if you're ever going to get stuff done, you've got to be able to do more than point out the problems. Furthermore, becoming the person who can effectively assess and solve problems requires you to be imaginative and open to a myriad of solutions. This is an invaluable skill and one that you will find to be helpful on your GSD Factor journey. This concept is like the culmination of dreaming big and never being satisfied. If you do those things, then you will find that solutions come much more freely than if not.

ACTIVITY

Identify a problem or opportunity in your life for which you can take the initiative to implement a solution or improvement. Write those possible solutions down, and share them with a trusted friend, mentor or adult. After sharing, consider implementing those possible solutions. Record your results.

_____

_____

_____

_____

_____

_____

_____

_____

_____

A SPACE TO DREAM BIG . . .

ACTION PLAN

HOW TO BE IMAGINATIVE

What does it look like to be imaginative in everyday life? It's a combination of all three sub-attributes: dreaming big, never being satisfied with the status quo, and using your imagination to develop and implement solutions. People who think like this are constantly looking for ways to improve. There is no problem that doesn't have a solution. Even when we don't know of a perfect solution, the goal of the imaginative GSDer is to work the problem. You may not find the right solution immediately, but imaginative thinking can transform you into a problem-solver that isn't afraid to try and fail quickly.

Though the solutions may be born of imagination and creativity, the thought process for finding the solution can easily be broken down into a few actionable steps:

1. Center yourself so you can open up to those big dreams and solutions. There are several practices that can be helpful for centering. Some people journal, color, exercise, create art, garden, etc. You can do whatever is necessary to get you to a place of peace and stability.

2. Ask questions. This is a part of never being satisfied. When it comes to dreams and ambitions, it pays to be inquisitive, curious, and constantly in search of knowledge. Ask yourself, how can I be better? Push for the next try-out, that next goal, strive for the academic or athletic level. Your ability to improve will directly affect your level of success. You cannot get better if you are not constantly looking for ways to *be* better.

3. Initiate. Remember *The Dog Poop Initiative*. It is one thing to dream-big and ponder all the possibilities for solutions and improvements, but the real challenge is taking the initiative to put all of these thoughts and considerations into practice. Will you be a problem-pointer or problem-solver?

As you make these steps of centering yourself to dream big and asking questions and initiating, you will become more comfortable with being imaginative, and soon those big dreams will begin to turn into your reality.

A Mantra for Being Imaginative

I dream big.

I dream big for myself.

I dream big for others.

I think about things differently.

I think about things creatively.

I think outside the box.

I push myself.

I am never satisfied.

There is no problem that I can't solve.

I am an innovative solutionist.

I initiate.

I take action.

I execute.

A SPACE TO DREAM BIG . . .

A SPACE TO DREAM BIG . . .

ATTRIBUTE FOUR

BE **PRESENT**

Being present means pausing and breathing
in the moment to bring oxygen to the brain,
stillness to the nervous system.
It means saying, "I'm here."

If you can't fly then run,
if you can't run then walk,
if you can't walk then crawl,
but whatever you do you have
to keep moving forward.

– MARTIN LUTHER KING JR.

ACTIVITY

Close your eyes and breathe for 30 seconds. How does that make you feel?

_____

_____

_____

_____

_____

_____

_____

_____

BE PRESENT

∞ O

THE WILLINGNESS TO KEEP SHOWING UP, DOING SOMETHING, AND LIVING WITH AN ATTITUDE OF PROGRESS AND NOT PERFECTION.

gsdfactor.com

KEEP SHOWING UP

In my life, there are a lot of areas where I have to focus on staying present and diligent, and many of these areas don't come naturally to me. What helps is that as a creative problem solver, I've learned that I will never get it right the first time, but if I keep showing up, I'll find power in the journey.

One of the areas I struggle with is being a present friend. I tend to slip into the coach or leader role easily. As a result, I don't have many personal friends, but I make a conscious effort to ensure that I am as present as possible with the friends I do have. Another area that I have to keep showing up for is in my rest. Though I am better at taking steps for self-care, I have difficulty doing *nothing* and pausing. I'm working on it, though. That is progress and proof that if we keep showing up, we will see improvement.

Showing up isn't just for ourselves. My daughter's karate school requires that even if you are not actively practicing on the mats, you still stand ready and present, showing up for your fellow teammates and cheering them on, because sometimes just being there is enough. That's showing up too. Sometimes all you have in you is to cheer on someone else, and when you can do that, you're showing up for that friend. After blowing my knee out and destroying any possibility of becoming a professional dancer, I made a decision to still show up for my students and co-workers at the dance school I helped co-found. Because of the severity of my injuries and the extra damage I did to my knee by continuing to dance on it for three more minutes after getting hurt, I had to wait six weeks before the doctors would do surgery. The doctors gave me a choice: those six weeks could either be spent on bed rest or in a wheelchair taking it easy. I spent them in the wheelchair, but I did not take it easy.

Instead, I showed up to class to finish out the year with my students. I taught as much as I could from the wheelchair, and when I couldn't teach or needed more help, my sister stepped in and demonstrated moves for me. It was a difficult six weeks, but that's what showing up for my students looked like. To this day, I cherish those days because they were the last days I spent as a teacher at that school. It was totally worth the challenge.

What happens when the odds are stacked against you? How do you keep showing up when it's feeling especially hard? Have you ever heard the idea that bullies operate from a deep underlying root of fear? What does a bully hate more than anything else? Bullies hate when people show up and stand up for themselves and for others. I've been there too. I returned to work after a break to a working environment that was clearly meant to isolate and antagonize me. I was faced with the option to show up or not. Even though I was removed from all of the projects I had been working on before I took leave, and even though I was removed from the leadership team and stopped from making any changes or decisions of impact, I still showed up to support my teammates when needed. I would give advice and support however I could. I would take time to coach and mentor others, and as a result, three coworkers that I mentored were able to use the guidance I shared to pivot into bigger and better positions.

Showing up even in the face of adversity or just meanness is a lesson that I'm already teaching my kids. I let them know that they may not make the team or get picked for the play, but they should still show up to cheer on their team and fellow classmates, because showing up isn't just for ourselves. Just like my daughter's karate school practices the same theory, we can easily apply this on a daily basis throughout our lives. This is what is remembered, and this mindset, when taught at a young age, can positively impact our world for generations to come.

I struggle with the concept of participation awards in events where there is a clear winner and loser, because in life, we win, and we lose. We get the spot on the roster, or we don't. Even when we lose, though, it's a character-building moment that teaches us that there will be losses in our lives, but that we must show up again.

ACTIVITY

Reflect on a recent mistake you made or an imperfection you've experienced. Make a list of ways you can extend yourself grace in that situation.

_____

_____

_____

_____

_____

_____

_____

_____

_____

_____

A SPACE TO DREAM BIG . . .

PROGRESS NOT PERFECTION

Attention, future GSDers! With all this talk about getting stuff done, it would be negligent of me not to warn you about one possible side-effect of GSDing. As you start building the motivation to be confident, imaginative, inquisitive, and now present, you might start feeling pressure to reach perfection. First of all, what is perfection? I think of perfection as the expectation that mistakes are unallowable and unacceptable. The desire to want to perform to perfection or to create perfect outcomes is human and has its benefits, like seemingly flawless product and performance executions. It would seem that since I have already discussed the need to keep showing up, perfection would be the obvious reason why one would need to do so. That couldn't be farther from the truth. Be careful, GSDers, that you are not pressuring yourself to keep showing up in the pursuit of perfection. That's a slippery slope. Instead, I'd like to challenge you to embrace the concept of *progress, not perfection.*

This is a much better goal post to target because it only requires you to be there. It's a given that anything you are doing will be excellent because you are already working on being confident, imaginative, and inquisitive. With attributes like that, the outcomes cannot be anything less than amazing. Perfectionism can be subtle, though, so make sure that you are exercising balance and realistic expectations when you show up. You do that by ensuring that you are constantly integrating rest and reevaluation into your routines. Know that being a work-in-progress is completely fine.

Sometimes showing up means just that. You just have to BE. Sometimes *being* looks well-put together, organized, and efficient. Other times, *being* looks broken and in a complete state of surrender, but the important part is that you are there. You are allowed to give yourself grace for those times. Perfectionists don't extend themselves grace. They don't celebrate the wins because the target is always moving. They are never satisfied, but not in the way that precipitates more knowledge and growth; they are never satisfied in a way that doesn't allow for a break or a self-congratulatory high-five. Resting and being in the moment are foreign concepts. This can lead to burnout, and I've been there.

ACTIVITY

Sometimes we think we have to do things perfectly to be successful, but that's not true. Rather than stress yourself to achieve perfection, focus on doing your best to complete your projects, tasks or goals. Once you do finish, ask yourself these two questions:

1. Did I complete this to the best of my ability?

2. Am I proud of myself?

If you can answer those two questions with a yes, consider that a success.

Now you try. Think of the most recent goal, task or project you had. Ask yourself those two questions and record the answers in the space below. If you answered "Yes," great. If you answered, "No," write what you could have done differently to get a yes to those questions. Either way, don't beat yourself up about it. Use the experience to strive for better for the next challenge.

Did I complete this to the best of my ability?   _____ Yes _____ No

If no, what could you have done differently?

_____

_____

Am I proud of myself?   _____ Yes _____ No

If no, what could you have done differently?

_____

_____

I've also had to learn over time that effort and output can be managed. What do I mean by this? When I need to give 100% then that's what I do. When I need to only give 80% then that's what I do.

GSDers have a tendency to be individuals who can beautifully manage their effort and output, being selective when they can give 80% or 100%. They are also highly efficient and effective producers which also means that a GSDer's 80% is a non GSDer's 100%. It's truly how we get so much stuff done.

It would be better for people who struggle with perfectionism, to simply get good with good enough. Get good with leaving things for the next day. Get good with laying out your to do list or initiatives into three buckets of NOW, NEXT, and LATER. There will always be something.

We have begun tapping into the concept of "good enough", but for now, let's focus on progress. *Webster's Dictionary* defines progress as "forward or onward movement toward a destination." Progress means you keep showing up. You are doing something, anything. You are moving forward even if it means a little. You just start even though you know it won't be the end result.

There are a couple of things you can do each day to make sure you keep moving forward. I've found that, as an entrepreneur, I need to make a few small, actionable steps each day like maintaining consistent communication with the necessary parties, be it via emails or text messages. I make sure things are filed away properly and that my social media and other online content is up-to-date. Again, the goal is progress, not perfection, and progress means trusting the process while you prepare for the opportunities that are coming.

Now that we have discussed the importance of progress over perfection and the significance of making small, actionable steps each day, let's address the elephant in the room. What do we do when things are not going as planned? We go back to the basics. We go back to where we started, making little steps and progress each day. We lean all the way in. We are methodical. We set our intentions daily. We celebrate the little wins.

ACTIVITY

What are some of your back-to-basics activities that are specifically grounding for you?

_____

_____

_____

_____

_____

_____

A business woman friend of mine talks about how the founder's or leader's mindset is so critical and important to entrepreneurial success. The founder's mindset is the set of foundational beliefs that serve you throughout your life. Many times, leaders have to come back to this mindset when they need to reset and refocus:

This mindset includes:

- Influence

- Zone of mastery

- Asking for help

Your influence reminds you of what impact you make to society. In moments of stress, ask yourself, "What is my reach and influence?"

Then, think about your zone of mastery: what are the skill sets that you have and do well? What is your superpower? What have you mastered along the way? Often, when we are going back to the basics, we can lean into our zone of mastery because it's well known, comfortable, and we are most confident doing those things.

Then finally, consider the art of asking for help. Learn to know when there is either a gap in your time and execution, your goals, or your skill sets. Believe that asking for help is a sign of strength and surrender. Even if you have a firm grasp on these ideas, you can be sure that you will still run into difficulties as a leader, specifically the temptation to be perfect. We must constantly remind ourselves that we are works in progress, and remember, it's progression over perfection.

ACTIVITY

Reflect on one area of your life where you tend to seek perfection. Identify specific, small, and consistent steps you can take to shift your focus towards progress not perfection. Come back to this section periodically to track your progress.

_____

_____

_____

_____

_____

_____

_____

A SPACE TO DREAM BIG . . .

⊣

BE PRESENT

My daughter plays softball, and recently, there weren't enough girls to make a team. Consequently, the coaches asked her if she wanted to join the boys team. Without hesitation she said, "Momma, you are the only girl on your work calls, and I want to be brave just like you. I want to play with the boys, and it's ok that I'm the solo girl on the baseball team." That comment hit me hard. What I realized was that she was watching. She was listening. She was observing. She was absorbing and taking bits and pieces of what she witnessed in my life and adapting them to her own life and experiences. Perhaps you are an older sibling or a mentor in your school. Remember: there are always eyes watching and ears listening.

Being present requires intentional awareness, and one way to be intentionally aware is to be an active listener. What does being an active listener mean? It's when you set intentions to hear the words, the purpose of the message, and the context surrounding it all. MindTools shares the following reasons that we listen:

- We listen to obtain information

- We listen to understand

- We listen for enjoyment

- We listen to learn

Another example of the importance of active listening is when you are receiving instructions. If your teacher or coach is giving you instructions for an assignment or a drill, and you only listen to the first part and start doing, you are likely going to miss some crucial steps to completing the task or at the very least completing it accurately. I use this phrase with my kids and clients alike: "slow down to speed up." If we rush through the listening process, we are going to miss critical details, but if we slow down and hear all the information, when it is time to go, you will be able to finish at great speed.

Are you practicing and modeling active listening in your conversations and behavior? What if you were to make a conscious effort to be present with active listening? How could it transform your GSD Factor life?

ACTIVITY

Share an example where you could leverage active listening in your life.

_____

_____

_____

_____

_____

_____

_____

_____

_____

_____

A SPACE TO DREAM BIG . . .

A SPACE TO DREAM BIG . . .

PIVOT DECISIONS

My earliest memory of having to make a pivot decision, a decision which completely changed the trajectory of my life, started at the age of sixteen. I was on my way to a professional dance career with our ballet company, training with some amazing dancers that would go on to the likes of Juilliard, Alvin Ailey, and Boston Conservatory. As the youngest member of the junior company by two years, my path was already taking a slightly different direction because of school, but my instructors, parents and I had a plan for me to graduate early to open the way for me to go to the Royal Ballet of Canada. Then I got sick, very sick.

For two years I didn't know what was wrong, but all of a sudden, my body and brain could no longer do the things that I had been trained to do. They wouldn't listen to the commands and muscle memory. After a long stretch of uncertainty, countless tests and doctors all over the South and Midwest, I was finally diagnosed with Lyme's disease. At this time, the research surrounding Lyme's disease was relatively new, and there wasn't much known about this debilitating, even life-threatening, disease. At the time of diagnosis, doctors gave me less than three months to live. My focus in life was no longer finishing ballet training in the studio for six plus hours per day, but in just trying to walk or swim in the pool.

After being diagnosed with Lyme's disease, I was quickly shifted from the pre-professional homeschool life familiar to many gymnasts and dancers. That's what the sport called for, but I now had to get accustomed to what I would classify as a normal life. What was this thing called high school? I wasn't sure, but I decided to fully embrace my junior and senior year by taking advanced classes, being elected as a class officer, enrolling in the theater program, volunteering with the younger students, and contributing to year end book projects. Whatever school had to offer, I was there for it.

ACTIVITY

Name a time in which you experienced one of life's pivots.

_____

_____

_____

_____

_____

_____

_____

_____

_____

_____

Some pivots in life present multiple lessons and nuggets, and it's important to lean into those lessons. Once my Lyme's disease was fully in remission, I was ready for my next pivot: co-founding a dance school. Just a year after opening up the dance school where I was feeding my love of dance by teaching and choreographing, life threw another curve ball at me. This one would require me to have four knee surgeries over the course of eighteen months. Are you kidding me? I had lost dance once. I pivoted my dream to teaching and choreography, got back into dance shape, and was performing with my students, which was such an honor. And for what? For it to be taken again?

My late father always said I had to have a backup plan, just in case. He was a two-time Rose Bowl-winning quarterback with Stanford University, but he also experienced countless injuries, which hindered his professional career. Consequently, he pivoted to the Air Force. Knowing my dad's journey and personal pivots taught me that no matter what life throws at you, you can pivot. You can find the next thing that brings you joy, peace, satisfaction, and fulfillment.

For many years, I had to find other outlets besides dance, and one of those outlets turned out to be coaching people. I love dreaming big with them. I live for the text message or call that says, "I have a problem. Can we chat?" I'm here for the good, bad, and tricky situations. I get joy from putting words to people's plans or mapping out the steps into action. It feels good to know that I helped someone do something amazing, or gave them key actions, steps, and a plan for what to do next. It's like a puzzle. You can either start at all the edges and move in, or start by finding the individual themes within and grouping it. You can approach it anyway you want or the best way for your brain, but the ultimate goal is to finish the puzzle. I like being there to help put that puzzle together. If those circumstances with my health and my injuries hadn't happened, I would not be sitting where I am today. You would not be reading this book. Those events, and how I allowed them to mold and shape me, opened up opportunities for the future.

There are times in everyone's life when we come to a decision point or crossroads where it is clear that there are two paths or two choices. Those are the pivot moments that can lead to reinvention and a whole different set of opportunities. In these circumstances, one may have to answer questions such as: Should I go left or go right? Should I move forward, or should I stop? Should I remain satisfied, or keep pushing? These decisions can be scary because of the uncertainty, but they can also be hugely successful and impactful if navigated effectively.

A SPACE TO DREAM BIG . . .

ACTION PLAN

HOW TO BE PRESENT

Being present may seem like a more passive GSD attribute, but the reality is that being present involves a great deal of intentionality. Think about it. All of the sub attributes in this section require constant consideration and adjustment of our perception. You cannot keep showing up; focusing on progress, not perfection; being present; or make pivot decisions if you are not consistently and intentionally thinking of doing all those things. The hardest part about consistently and intentionally being present by maintaining all four of these sub attributes is the risk of falling into perfectionism. If you find that you lean on the side of perfectionism, or you are a recovering perfectionist, here are some actionable steps you can take to be present without being a perfectionist.

1. Keep showing up. Create a list of small, go-to steps that will ensure you keep showing up which means being present, even if for a moment. It's the art of doing something–anything, and trusting that process, even when it seems that there are more pivots than plans. Your small steps can include things like a daily gratitude journal or a check-in with a work-out partner. Whatever the steps are, they will be unique to your lifestyle and should be tailored to whatever you need to keep you in a state of awareness to keep showing up.

2. Extend yourself grace. This is more of an informal step, but it's still important. Make sure you are reminding yourself that the focus is progress not perfection and that, therefore, you will mess up. You will make mistakes. The key is to accept wherever you are in your process, so that it's easier for you to commit to taking a step, any step, forward.

3. Celebrate your wins. As a recovering perfectionist, I now appreciate the fact that progress is good enough. Moving the needle, accomplishing one task, or doing one thing for ourselves should be celebrated. Take the time to do that. It can be as small as a verbal, "Good job" to yourself, or as big as throwing a party when you reach your goals. Whatever the accomplishment, acknowledge it and celebrate it.

4. The commitment to being present requires a change in mindset, reminding us to be actively aware of recordings that are playing in our heads, and when our minds wander, we must reset, be it with meditation, music, or spoken word. Being present also means remembering one of the simplest of things–to breathe. I have a picture on my desk of two beautifully painted lungs that simply says, "Inhale, exhale." Bring it back to your breath. It will bring clarity. It will slow down your heart rate. It will steady the emotions. It will bring stillness to your nervous system.

Finally, being present requires an ever-present attitude of gratitude for progress not perfection. It's great to get all the things done, but this attribute allows you to be grateful and accepting of the times when you don't.

A Mantra for Being Present

I am still.

I breathe in.

I am silent.

I breathe out.

I am present.

I am at peace.

I show up for me.

I show up for others.

I am enough.

I am a beautiful work in progress.

I move forward.

I am one with my breath.

I am exactly where I need to be.

A SPACE TO DREAM BIG . . .

A SPACE TO DREAM BIG . . .

ATTRIBUTE FIVE

○○●

BE **RESILIENT**

Being resilient means inhabiting a mental strength and superpower of perseverance in the face of doubt.

"

Hardships often prepare ordinary people for an extraordinary destiny.

– C.S. Lewis

"

ACTIVITY

Complete this sentence:

"I, _____ (Insert name here) am resilient.

I am a force to be reckoned with. I love myself. I am bold. I am brave.

I am brilliant. My voice is my strongest weapon."

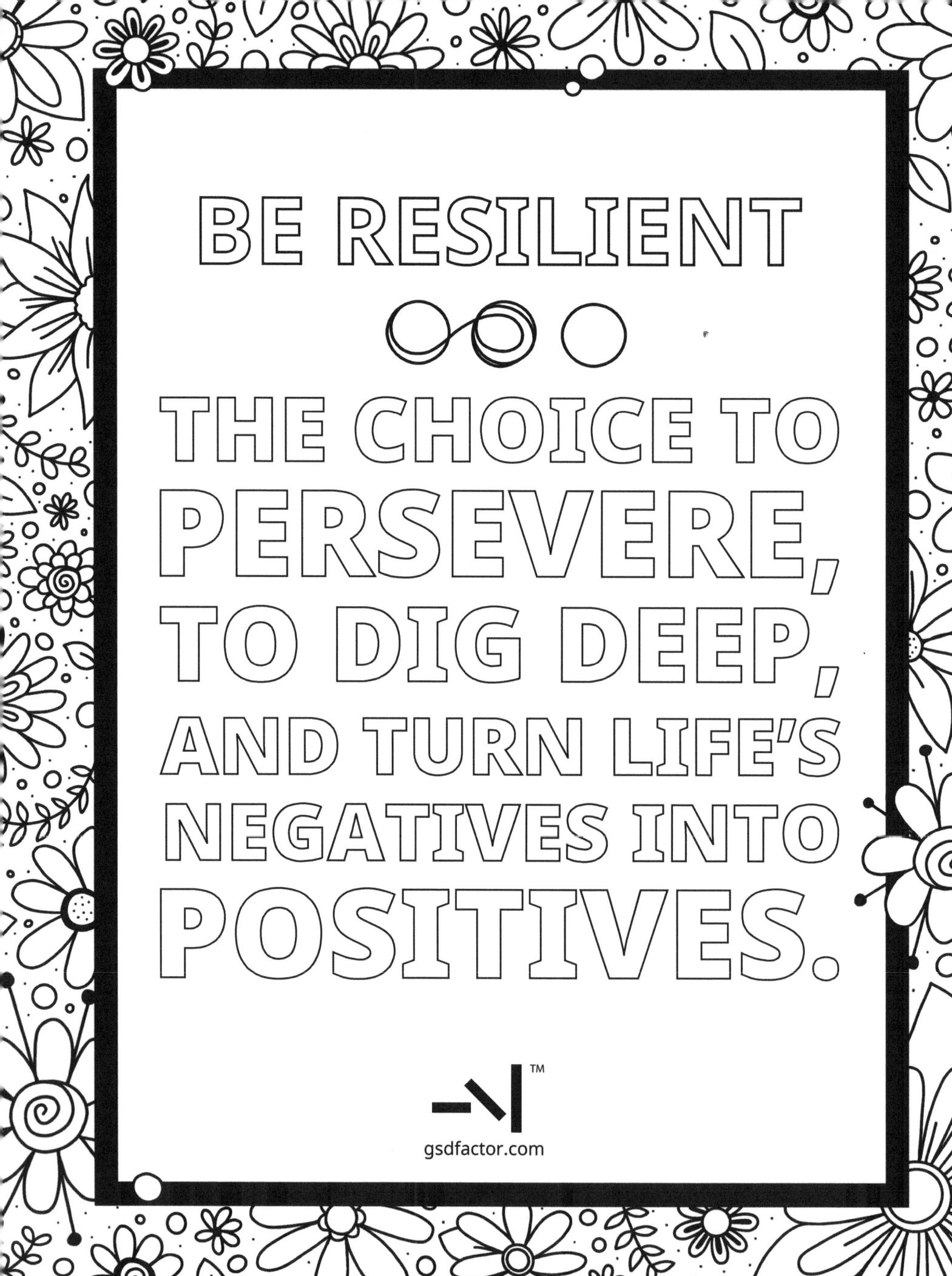

BE RESILIENT

THE CHOICE TO PERSEVERE, TO DIG DEEP, AND TURN LIFE'S NEGATIVES INTO POSITIVES.

gsdfactor.com

RESILIENT LIFE

Throughout this book, I've talked about the power of showing up, pivoting, and learning something from every situation. All these lessons are driving towards the GSD Factor attribute of being resilient.

Being resilient is about having an attitude that says life can be tough, with days that are good and days that are bad, but the sun rises in the morning.

Resilience requires honest acknowledgment of where you are. In order to be resilient, you have to be authentic with yourself and your current circumstances. Part of being resilient is knowing that when you are knocked down, it's okay to sit, cry, yell, scream, or do whatever you need to do in that moment. Those feelings need to get out. We are human, and we all feel things. That's how we were created. Resilience is not pushing down those feelings of sadness or anger but holding them, honoring them and then letting them go. We hold space for them for as long as they still serve us. We are present with them as long as it takes to get it out of our system. That's what you need, but then, you rise from the ashes. You get back up.

Think about a loss you have experienced in your life or a traumatic event or situation that robbed you of something? Have you given yourself permission to grieve it? Have you even talked about it? I have found, in these moments, that the sooner I talk, cry, yell or scream out my frustrations, the sooner my head, heart, and emotions all come back into alignment to be present and face the grief, sorrow, anger, and injustice head-on.

ACTIVITY

Reflect on a challenging experience you have gone through and how you have grown from it. What feelings come up as you are thinking and writing? Have you talked to someone about it?

_____

_____

_____

_____

_____

_____

_____

_____

_____

Athletes are some of the best at showing us how to live life with resilience. They often reflect on wins and losses. They study footage and tape to see what they did wrong, so they can learn and not make the same mistake again. In business, we call this process "retrospect." It's during this time that we ask the tough questions. What went wrong? What could we have done better, and what can we do better moving forward?

Applying the process of retrospecting to life will help you see that we never reach a finished level while living a resilient life. Resilience is one of those things upon which we can continue to grow and improve. It's one of the first lessons we learn when we are born, and it can be one of the final lessons before you move on from this life. Each day can be a lesson in resilience. Each time you find yourself in a circumstance asking, "What can I learn from this? What can I learn to do versus not to do," that's you exercising your resilience muscle. That's how you grow and expand your resilience and stamina. The next time something comes up, an experience with bullying, a life-threatening illness, a hard exam, whatever it is, your resilience muscle memory will kick in, and it will become a little easier to bounce back.

Being resilient is the GSD Factor attribute and life skill of knowing that even though we have to go through things in life, we can learn something, and we can help somebody else by sharing that lesson. As we are walking out that journey, it is becoming a part of our story. A story that can be shared with others. A story that brings change. A story that brings hope.

ACTIVITY

Think of moments of resilience that you have experienced in your life. Now gather small containers, such as shoe boxes or jars, and a variety of art supplies. Create a time capsule that represents your journey of resilience. You can include objects, notes, drawings, or any other meaningful items that symbolize your resilience, such as quotes, photos, or mementos. Afterward, share what you included in your time capsule and why, reflecting on your resilient experiences and the significance of the items you chose.

_____

_____

_____

_____

_____

_____

_____

_____

A SPACE TO DREAM BIG . . .

A SPACE TO DREAM BIG . . .

TRUST THE TIMING

Much of what we've discussed as it pertains to the GSD Factor attributes and sub attributes has been dependent on parts of our lives that we can control. You can control how you show up in the world by being confident. You can control how much you know by being inquisitive. You can control how you handle problems by being imaginative and how you react to life's curveballs by being present. Being resilient also has an element of personal control in that you have to make a choice to continue to get up after being knocked down, but there is an element of uncertainty that exists within this GSD Factor attribute that doesn't necessarily show up in others: timing. No matter how confident, inquisitive, imaginative or present we are in any situation, if the timing isn't right, it's not happening. That's what makes resilience so important and sometimes challenging. Being resilient also means being aware that we cannot control timing, but we must trust it.

What does it look like to trust the timing? Though we can't control timing, we aren't just passively experiencing time. So let's talk about how we manage the time we have. When you look at your life with school, family, friends, extracurricular activities, you probably have to juggle and make sure there is enough time for all of it.

Regardless of all the responsibilities you may have, you have to take care of yourself first. Consider this: what we give to others comes from what we give to ourselves. Furthermore, if we haven't made time to give ourselves rest, love, grace, patience, etc., where are we going to find it to give to others? Your family, your team, your friend, and you are all counting on you. If you aren't able to be there, those things don't function the way they are intended to. Now, that doesn't mean that you can't ever not be there. It means that if you are not there, it should not be as a result of your lack of self-care. Managing our time to include self-care requires balance. That's the real issue. Remember we are striving for school-work-life-family integration and that includes self-care.

ACTIVITY

Recount an experience in which timing affected your life. Looking back on that experience, are you grateful for how things happened? Why or why not?

_____

_____

_____

_____

_____

When you evaluate your workload, think about what progress, not perfection, looks like. I'm always evaluating what needs to be done, and I always have a list. One of my employees shared that she categorizes her personal and professional life into three buckets:

- NOW – These are the items that need to be addressed immediately. You might get to them today or tomorrow, but getting them done is critical.

- NEXT – These are the items that may be completed tomorrow or this week. They are a close follower after the "now" items but aren't the most pressing.

- LATER – These are the items that you have a little more time to ideate and plan. They could be addressed next week, next month or next quarter, etc.

ACTIVITY

Think about the tasks in your life that you need to complete. List out your top 3 Now, Next, and Later tasks.

NOW

1. _____

2. _____

3. _____

NEXT

1. _____

2. _____

3. _____

LATER

1. _____

2. _____

3. _____

However you decide to group your long to-do list, and whatever timing buckets you use, just know that your entire list doesn't all have to be completed today, and that you may not be able to do it all alone. Ask for help. Along with admitting that I'm not the smartest person in the room, I also remind myself that I'm not expected to get it all done today. We must remember to extend ourselves grace.

I know what you're thinking. Time management is great. Getting help is awesome, but what happens when life starts throwing curveballs? Well, that's when we have to learn to trust the timing. Athletes and dancers have an incredible sense of timing – timing of movements, timing of breathing, timing of sequence.

Let's use football as an example: Reading the defense in football is much like reacting to the challenges and uncertainties of life. Sure, there may be a plan, but maybe life is throwing us something for which we weren't prepared, forcing us to call an audible. An audible is a football term for when the quarterback has already given the offense a play in the huddle, but right before it's time to execute, the quarterback senses a shift in the defense's strategy. As a result, the quarterback makes an executive decision to change plays to face this new strategy. That happens all the time in real life. We make plans as well as we can, and suddenly life shifts those plans. Then, like quarterbacks, we have to pause, re-evaluate, and re-execute.

In keeping with the football analogy, I can say that throughout my life, there have been many instances where the defense blitzed, executing a sudden and intense attack, causing me to call an audible. In some cases, I had to pause, re-evaluate, and re-execute. Life has taught me the importance of being agile. By looking at the past, retrospectively, I can see how it prepared me for the future. Get good with change. Change is healthy. Change means that you are growing and evolving.

When you are thinking through strategic timing you must have a vision that is fueling that passion. That vision is your map. Even when the timing seems off or the strategy needs to be changed, your vision remains. Part of having that solid vision is having the foundation of knowing who you are and what you want out of life. That is your compass. That is your constant.

Perhaps another lesson to be learned from trusting the timing is whether your vision can stand the pressure of the seasons of uncertainty. Can your vision stand the test of time? Can it stand adversity? Can it stand the failures and successes? When timing and vision are being challenged or refined, that is a great opportunity to determine whether you should do or be. Ask yourself, "Do I need to push or pull during this period?" Only you truly know what you need as you are walking out your journey. Trusting the timing is an important part of this attribute, because it also requires you to trust yourself. You have to trust in your own management of the time you have been given, and trust that you have prepared as much as you possibly can for those unexpected twists and turns of life. No matter how many times you get knocked down, trust the timing. Trust yourself and get back up. Eventually, you'll walk right into your success.

ACTIVITY

The first timeline is of your life, marking important events, challenges, and achievements. Reflect on how past experiences, both good and bad, have shaped your journey and prepared you for the future.

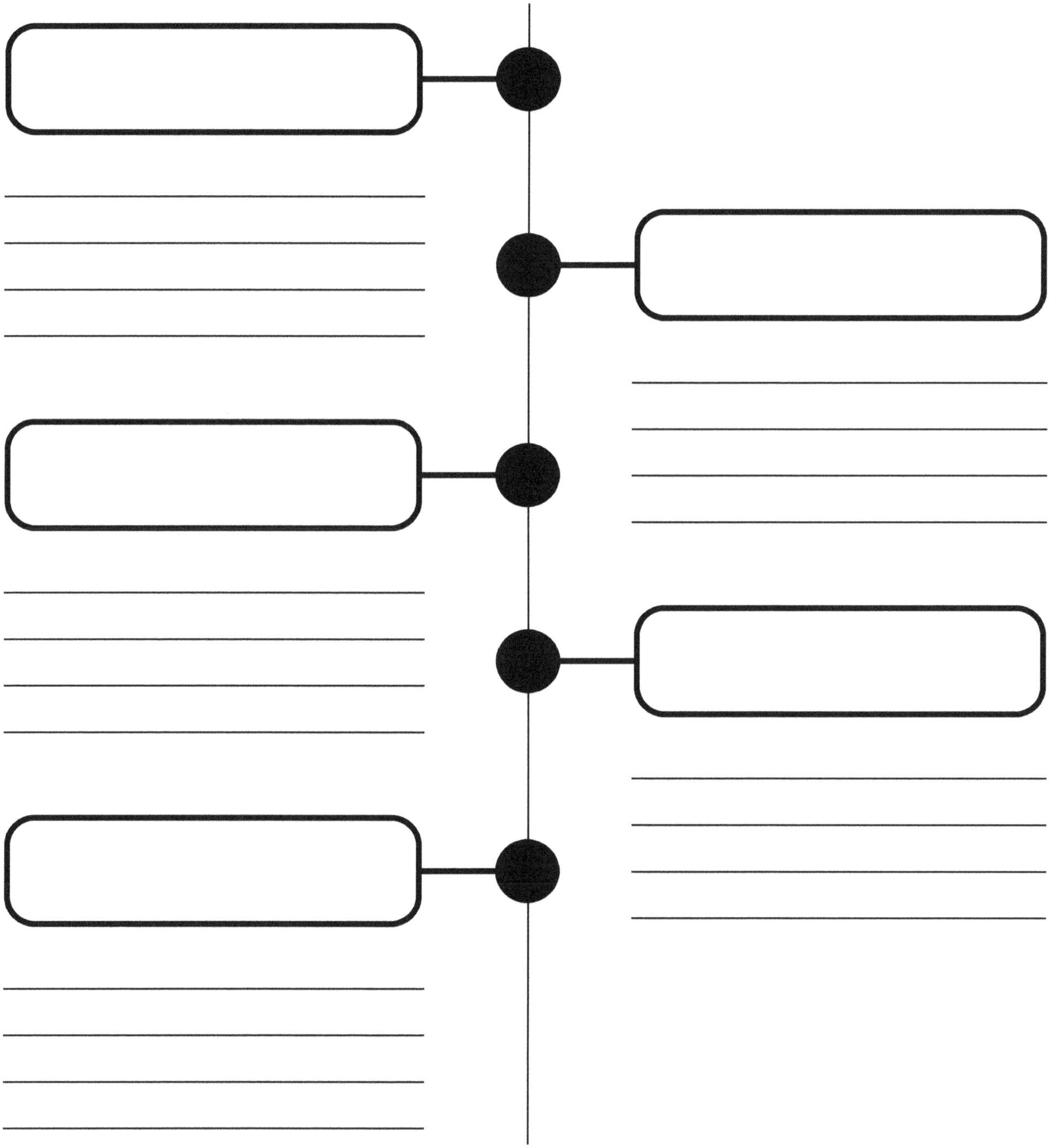

The second timeline is of your future. Leave plenty of space between events and consider that there may be many challenges, detours and situations that pop up along the way. Also consider that those future experiences will help mold and shape you the same way the experiences in your past have molded you up until now.

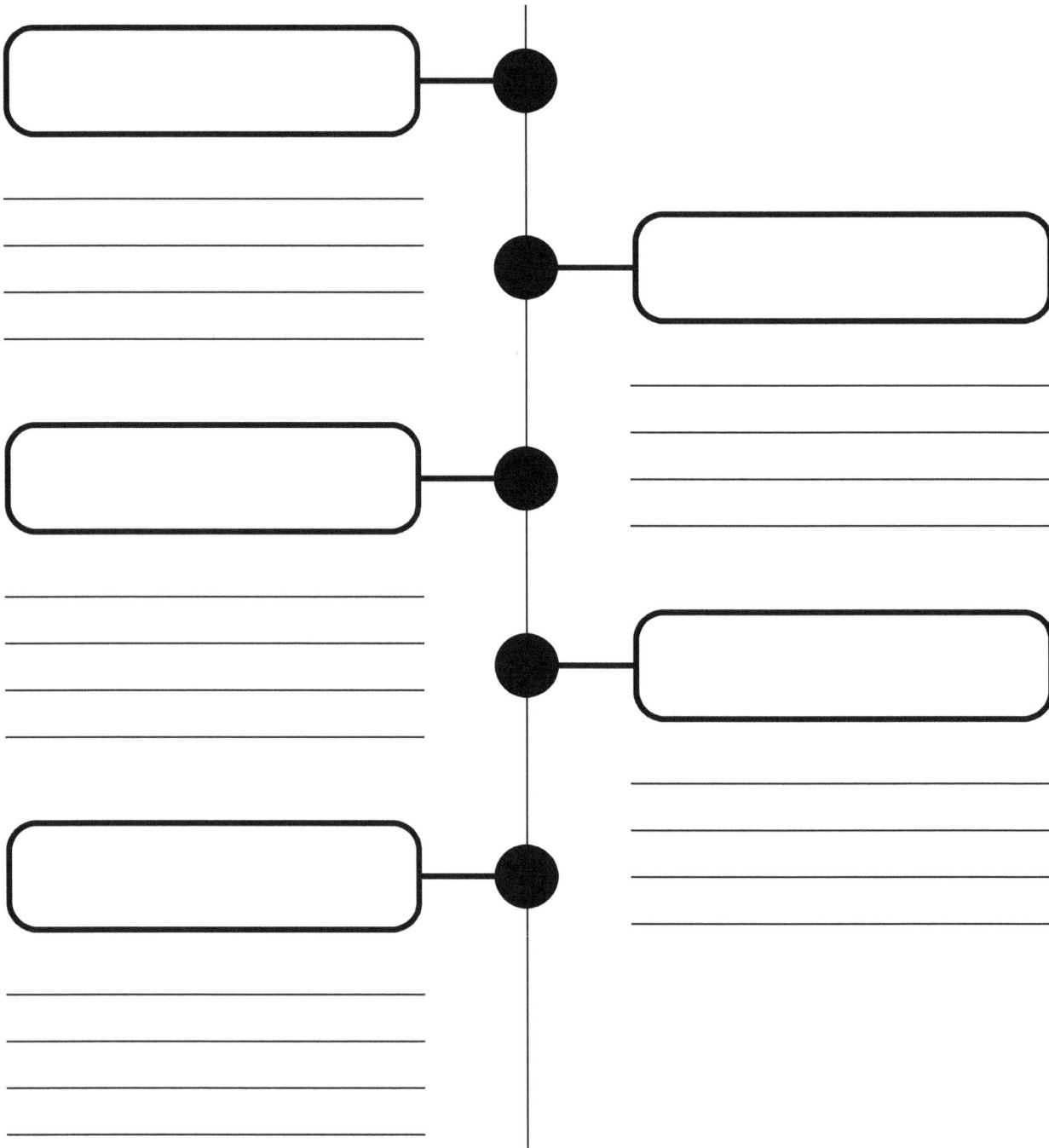

A SPACE TO DREAM BIG . . .

A SPACE TO DREAM BIG . . .

PERSPECTIVE

Have you ever met or known someone whose presence can brighten up the room they walk into? They offer a different point of view on things, large or small. I call them "breath-of-fresh-air" people. These people provide balance by providing another way to look at things.

Perspective is the way we see life and the experiences it brings. Perhaps you have had a tough time in life with family or your health. That daily battle can bring perspective or perseverance like nothing else. It cuts through the stuff and forces you to see and acknowledge what truly matters. Perspective lessons at any young age shape you, mold you.

To those of you who are, perhaps, on a journey where you have to exercise your perseverance every day, I see you. I hear you. I'm cheering you on. Your GSD community is cheering you on. Your ability to be resilient is directly related to how you see the struggles and challenges you may face. I challenge you to consider the concept of perspective lessons the next time you find yourself in a difficult situation. It may be hard, but think about how much wiser you are going to be on the other side. Don't let it rattle you. You've got this.

ACTIVITY

I call this activity, the Glass Half-Full Exercise. Think about a situation in your life that didn't go exactly how you would have wanted. Write in the top of the jar what didn't go right and write in the bottom of the jar what did go right.

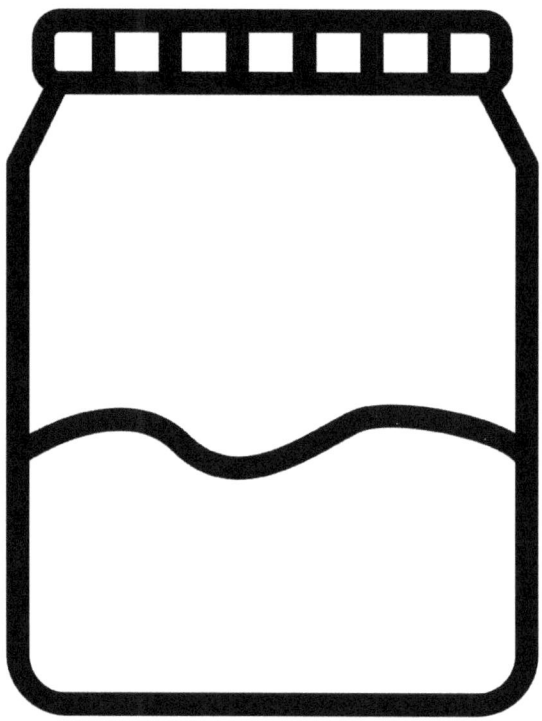

Then complete the sentence below to help you see that situation with a more positive perspective.

_____ didn't go as I would have liked,

but _____

Here's an example:
    The class election didn't go as I would have liked, but campaigning gave me more confidence when meeting new people.

A SPACE TO DREAM BIG . . .

ACTION PLAN

HOW TO BE RESILIENT

Living out a resilient life takes sheer will. It requires grit. It requires you to dig deep. Resilience requires the stamina and perseverance to acknowledge that life can be tough sometimes, but also leaves room to acknowledge the moments for learning and growth. Many times, people will ask me for advice on how to be resilient. It's no simple process, but in attempting to reduce resilience to a series of actionable items, I suggest several things:

- Take time to feel your feels. You are a human, not a robot. Sometimes you need to get that raw emotion out.

- Keep a level-headed mindset, one that is open to seeing your situation from a different perspective. Remember those perspective lessons, and try to remain aware that whatever the situation is, there may be another way to look at it and learn.

- Ensure that as you experience hardship, you remain present in body, mind, soul, and emotion. No matter what hardships you are experiencing, you can still experience joy, happiness and love in those challenging times as well, as long as you stay present and open to it.

Be sure to maintain your perspective by walking with humility and gratitude. Think about what you will be able to share with others at the end of this journey and be grateful that you made it to the other side to be able to share the wisdom you have gained. Think about how this weaves itself into your story. You are extraordinary. You are resilient. You are destined for great things.

A Mantra for Being Resilient

I am resilient.

I matter.

I am a force to be reckoned with.

I love myself.

I am bold.

I am brave.

I am brilliant.

My voice is my strongest weapon.

I am courageous.

I am valiant.

I am strong.

I am extraordinary.

I am destined for great things.

A SPACE TO DREAM BIG . . .

ATTRIBUTE SIX

○○●

BE **INFLUENTIAL**

Being influential means being a leader.
It's about knowing when to listen and when to act.

"

If you want to change the world,
start with yourself.

– Mahatma Gandhi

"

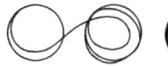

ACTIVITY

List the top five characteristics you think a good leader should have.

_____

_____

_____

_____

_____

_____

_____

_____

LEADER BY EXAMPLE

What does being a leader mean to you? There are countless examples of leadership all around us: good leaders, bad leaders, young leaders, old leaders, leaders who had great wisdom, and leaders who didn't make the best decisions. To me, being a leader is about knowing when to listen and when to act. It's about showing up. GSD Factor leaders are present and authentic. They know when they need to lead, when to follow, when to push, and when to support.

Being a leader can also be lonely at times. Leaders have to make tough decisions. Perhaps you already know this. You might be the captain of your sports team or the lead musician in the orchestra. Your coach or music instructor might look to you to lead your fellow classmates and teammates. When you are assigned this task, first actively listen to all parties, taking into consideration their views or thoughts. Now, armed with information from both sides, you will have to make the best decision with the information you have at that moment considering everyone involved. Decisions like this may or may not be popular, but this isn't a popularity contest. It's a character building exercise that is training you on the art of being a leader.

ACTIVITY

What is the toughest decision you have had to make?

_____

_____

_____

_____

What was the outcome of that decision? Do you still think your choice was right? Why or why not?

_____

_____

_____

_____

Being a leader calls for a level of courage like no other. Sometimes it means standing in for your team or classmates. Sometimes it even means mustering your courage to stand in front of bullies and defend the underdog.

For those who are aspiring to be leaders, we need you. We need leaders who walk with authentic conviction, who actively listen, who have empathy. We need leaders who know when and how to take action, who can encourage and empower, who seek equality. We need leaders who give back to their communities. We need leaders who are thinking about the next generation and preparing those future leaders to stand on their predecessors' shoulders. Remember, leadership is not for the faint of heart. It has its challenges, but it is also so rewarding.

The biggest lessons that I've learned from being a leader is conviction and confidence in my decisions and my willingness to exhibit humility. When I make a decision, I do so unapologetically. I stick to it no matter the peer pressure I may receive. When I say no, it is a full sentence, and I do so without apology. However, I'm willing to acknowledge when I have made a mistake or something has gone awry. I'm a human, and therefore, not impervious to making mistakes.

My goal as a leader has always been to stand up and protect those under me, whether they were employees, team members, or family; I was their advocate. I made sure to show up for my team. For my classmates. For my sister.

Being a professional in the technology space, I have had the honor of working with many international teams, which exposed me to a beautiful tapestry of culture, traditions, and faiths. When managing transformation projects that are powered by international teams, you must consider and account for all the major national and faith-based holidays in the project plan. This can get very tricky, especially during the fourth quarter of the year.

On one particular project, my client was both U.S. and U.K. based, but as with any transformation project, we had teams located in the U.S., Canada, U.K., Europe, and India. The client only wanted to observe the U.S. and U.K. holidays, but wanted the employees and team members based in the other countries to keep working so as not to slow down the project. When the other holidays were brought up, the client refused to allow them to be observed. As one of the transformation leaders, I immediately spoke up on behalf of all my team, no matter where they lived or what faith they practiced. In a massive project planning meeting, I outlined the project policy that all national and faith based holidays would be observed by those project team members, regardless of their location or practice. We had planned for this in the project timeline, and it was imperative that we respected all team members as equal outside of ethnicity, faith, gender, or otherwise.

The client was taken aback that I had pushed back. The teams were taken aback that I had stood up for them., but when it came to the holidays that were planned for, the teams showed up. They worked a little extra ahead of the holidays, communicated effectively to the teams that would continue to be working in another part of the world, and then worked a little more when they returned to get back up to speed.

Being a leader, at times, calls for pushing your team to excellence or raising them to the next level of growth. Effective leadership means pushing your team, rolling up your sleeves and saying, "What can I do to help?" Perhaps for you, it's a school project, a scout project, or a sports team training for a tournament. Whatever it may be, be the leader by getting in the trenches to help, support, and encourage.

ACTIVITY

What leadership traits do you already have?

_____

_____

_____

_____

_____

What traits do you want to develop to be a better leader in the future?

_____

_____

_____

_____

_____

What are three, concrete steps you can take now to start developing those traits?

_____

_____

_____

_____

_____

_____

_____

_____

_____

_____

_____

_____

A SPACE TO DREAM BIG . . .

↘|

CHALLENGING THE STEREOTYPES

Have you ever been misunderstood or experienced having someone make a wrong assumption about you? This can be a very lonely and painful place to be in. Someone's thoughts or perceptions of you are not the true picture of who you are. Oftentimes people think they know best, and they think they can tell what kind of person someone is by their clothes, how they walk, what they say. This simply isn't true.

As a senior in high school, there was a guy who wanted to ask me out, but when he learned of my career aspirations and lack of interest in immediately becoming a "Mrs.," he quickly ended things. I can still recall a conversation we had on the back of his truck when he asked, "Don't you want to get married and take on someone else's name?" to which I responded, "I do want to get married, at some point, but I won't be losing my maiden name. I will hyphenate." He replied, "Is that allowed?"

Sidenote: I guess it is, because here I am, years later, a happily married woman, mother, multiple business owner, and author with a hyphenated last name! That guy made the mistake of thinking that because I was a girl, I must only care about being a wife. I did want that, but that wasn't all I wanted. He made a hasty judgment, like many people do.

My first challenge to you is this: don't judge a book by its cover. Take a moment to pause; then introduce yourself so that you are getting first-hand information. Then ask questions, but more importantly, listen. You would be amazed at what you can learn. You never know–you may be surprised to meet a new friend.

My second challenge to you is to continue to be your true authentic self. You may win some friends and lose some friends, but remember no one can be *everyone's* friend. Surround yourself with positive, happy people that align with your life principles. You are a GSDer, someone who gets stuff done with confidence, inquisitiveness, imagination, presence, resilience, and influence and doesn't worry about what people think. Live your unicorn life.

A SPACE TO DREAM BIG . . .

HEROES + SHEROES + MENTORS

We should always be showing gratitude and thanks for the mentors and heroes in our lives. Hopefully, we all have heroes and mentors, those that have inspired us. These are the people that have impacted us, who have seen something special in us when we did not see it in ourselves. I have been blessed with many of these people throughout my life.

The first shero I want to thank is someone I call my Warrior Princess. Her energy was amazing. When we met, we found an immediate synergy–a sisterly bond in empowering women of our varying generations. Our visions and our dreams were aligned. She was what some might call a jack of all trades. She was an artist, musician, entrepreneur, mentor, and leader who had a heart for investing in her community, specifically into other African American women. To put it lightly, she was a powerhouse. It was like she saw no limits. She dreamed even bigger than I do, and that's saying a lot?

My next great mentor is my Fairy Godmother who helped my career trajectory and was a critical piece to my transition from a small business into the corporate world. She was a trailblazing recruiter in the Nashville area and was one of the founding members of a staffing company that went on to gain national renown. She redefined how you recruit someone but also how you recruit for them. She considered herself an advocate who needed to get to know the candidate in order to come along beside them, tell their story, and get them placed in a career. She looked at a girl and saw the potential woman I could be. She saw my big personality that just got stuff done, and she said, "YES! I can use that."

From her perspective and seat as a recruiter, she could mold me, train me, and prepare me. Fairy Godmother started by teaching me the STAR methodology and how it applies to answering questions. These questions could be for school interviews, job interviews, or general problem solving:

STATE the situation.

List out the **T**ASKS.

Explain the **A**CTION items.

Share the **R**ESULTS.

And finally, as I was writing this book, I learned that heaven gained one of my angel sheroes who I considered to be a spiritual mother. She had a profound impact on my personal life these last 17 years. Her wisdom and spiritual guidance guided me through many of life's milestones. She was steadfast and faithful in her check ins and encouragement even as her health faltered.

I share this as an encouragement to reach out to your heroes, sheroes and mentors in your life to thank them. Be intentional and be present; let them hear from you. Share with them the impact they have made on your life.

ACTIVITY

Who is a mentor in your life and why?

_____

_____

_____

_____

_____

Have you told them?

_____

_____

_____

_____

_____

If you don't yet have a mentor, take some time to think about the people in your life who may be good mentors, especially those who seem to have some of the same qualities you think a good leader should have. This may feel a little uncomfortable to you, but if you already have a relationship with any of these people, consider asking them if they would be willing to share some of their wisdom and expertise with you. If you don't know them, don't yet have a relationship with them, or are not yet comfortable asking for that level of guidance right now, consider researching some historical or well-known figures who may have or had leadership qualities you admire. There may be biographies or memoirs of their lives that will be informative and inspiring concerning how to be influential.

ACTION PLAN

HOW TO BE A LEADER

Part of being a GSDer, of having the GSD Factor, is being a leader. To me, being a leader is about knowing when to listen and when to act.

Leadership is not for the faint of heart. It can be lonely but rewarding. Most often, you have to lead by example, and as we get older and look to the future, we also bring the next generation alongside us. We mentor them, so they can stand on our shoulders. From my experience, you feel real success when you can see your mentees trailblazing, breaking glass ceilings, and going beyond your wildest dream big for them.

As a leader and a GSDer, challenge injustice, give voice to the under-voiced, and stand for equality. While bringing along the next generation, honor those that have gone before you– your mentors, your heroes, and your sheroes. Thank them for paving the way. Identify what kind of leader you want to be or aspire to be and do that. Live that. Find a mentor that speaks to your true authentic self and who makes courage resonate within you. Above all be who YOU are and get stuff done. That's it. It's that simple.

A Mantra for Being Influential

I am a leader.

I am bold.

I am courageous.

I am brave.

I amplify.

I lift up.

I push.

I support.

I speak with truth.

I speak with respect.

I listen.

I honor.

I am humble.

A SPACE TO DREAM BIG . . .

A SPACE TO DREAM BIG . . .

THE GSD FACTOR LIFE

Recently, I was watching *Frozen 2* with my tiny humans, and the song "Show Yourself" seemed to speak to me like never before. The whole premise of the song basically asserts that whatever it is that you are looking for to give you validation or permission to succeed can only be found in you. You are the answer to your questions. You are the one you have been waiting for. That's what I want you to take away from this book.

All of the attributes we've discussed in this book–being Confident, Inquisitive, Imaginative, Present, Resilient, and Influential–are all parts of the GSD Factor life.

I have told you what worked for me, the attributes that I found to have encouraged and transformed me, but ultimately, the action behind each attribute is your responsibility. You have to do the work for yourself. You have to show up. You have to decide which tools you are adding to your toolbox.

Being a GSDer will cause others to look to you for guidance. It is inevitable, because once all these attributes are working in your life, people are going to notice that you get stuff done. Then, they are going to start watching you and maybe even asking you how you do it.

Here is my final challenge for you: How do you apply these attributes to your life?

You may decide after reading this that you are good with where you are, and that is okay. However, I hope that after reading this, there is something inside you saying, "I want to get stuff done." When that happens, know that you've got this. You are not alone. You have taken that first step to say, "I am here. Hear my voice. Know my name. Watch as I write history for the next generation. Witness my story, my journey."

Now, let's get stuff done!

A SPACE TO DREAM BIG . . .

www.ingramcontent.com/pod-product-compliance
Lightning Source LLC
Chambersburg PA
CBHW051851140626
46547CB00034BA/3060